Second E

Figure It Out
How I Learned to Live Without Digits in a Digital World

To Ashley

"Pour It Out"

Mark Speckman
with
W. Jason Niedermeyer

Mark Speckman

©2015 Coaches Choice. Second edition. All rights reserved. Printed in the United States.

No part of this book may be reproduced, stored in a retrieval system or transmitted, in any form or by any means, electronic, mechanical, photocopying, recording, or otherwise, without the prior permission of Coaches Choice. Throughout this book, the masculine shall be deemed to include the feminine and vice versa.

ISBN: 978-1-60679-331-2
Library of Congress Control Number: 2014960179
Book layout: Cheery Sugabo
Cover design: Cheery Sugabo
Front cover photo: Rogerio Photographe

Coaches Choice
P.O. Box 1828
Monterey, CA 93942
www.coacheschoice.com

Dedication

To Sue—
Figuring out how to get her to marry me is my greatest achievement

Acknowledgments

I would like to thank several people for their help in making this book a reality. I'd like to thank Jason Niedermeyer for his work getting the stories from my mind and onto the page. I'd like to thank Dr. Jim Peterson and his staff at Coaches Choice for their work laying out the book, as well as serving as a general sounding board—without their dedication, this book wouldn't have gotten finished. I'd like to thank Frank Schuman, whose patience through the printing process was more than anyone, especially me, could have expected.

In addition to the people who worked directly on the book, there are so many friends, co-workers, players, and teammates who have helped shape my life. Because to try to mention them all, without leaving a few deserving ones off, would be an impossible task, I won't attempt to. Please know that I appreciate each and every one of you more than words can express. With that being said, I would be remiss in not giving a special thanks to Don Brock and Chris Lueder, for their longstanding and consistent friendship and counsel.

Finally, I'd like to thank my family—you have been the driving force in my life. I'll start with my parents, Jan and the late Don Speckman. Their wisdom, insight, and courage in raising me, without having a clue on how to approach a no-handed child, was remarkable. Thanks for helping me succeed and even more importantly, letting me fail. My siblings, Mike, Matt, and Mary, have been friends, teachers, and patient onlookers as I was often given the spotlight over them. Thanks for a lifetime of help and support. My son Tim, and step-daughters Lisa and Julie have made my heart swell with pride with each accomplishment—and each day it continues to grow. And lastly, a big thank you to my wife Sue, my best friend. She has allowed me to pursue my dreams and supported me every step of the way. She has been the centerpiece of this journey, the gravitational pull that never allows me to stray (too far anyway). The woman is a force of nature who positively affects everyone's life she touches—her students, her children, and her husband. Thank you for committing your life to living with a guy who is still trying to *figure out* how he got so lucky.

Contents

Dedication 3
Acknowledgments 4
Preface 6
Chapter 1: Tiny Tim 11
Chapter 2: Look Ma, No Hands! 13
Chapter 3: Captain Hook 16
Chapter 4: Not Your Average Show and Tell 19
Chapter 5: The Great Equalizer 23
Chapter 6: The Word Is "*Hand*icapped," Not "*Hook*icapped" 29
Chapter 7: Remember the ~~Titans~~ Mighty Scots 38
Chapter 8: The Long Road to College 44
Chapter 9: I Made It! (Now What Do I Do?) 54
Chapter 10: Ball and Band: The Life of a Football-Playing Musician 60
Chapter 11: Life, Liberty, and the Pursuit of Gainful Employment 65
Chapter 12: This Is What You Call Gainful Employment? 73
Chapter 13: So That's It ... I'm a Football Coach 77
Chapter 14: Welcome to the Big Time (in California) 84
Chapter 15: I Already Knew Life Wasn't Perfect, but Thanks for the Reminder 88
Chapter 16: There's a First Time for Everything 93
Chapter 17: The Snowball Effect 99
Chapter 18: Is It Getting Hot in Here? (I Don't Know, but That Snowball Sure Looks Like It's Melting) 109
Chapter 19: How Long Did It Take Sisyphus to Figure It Out? 114
Chapter 20: The Grass Is Always Greener ... or Is It? 120
Chapter 21: Still Figuring It Out 126

Epilogue 129
Appendix: Photos Through the Years 133
About the Authors 143

Preface

I have always been different. I have been made aware of it since my earliest recollections. Each day the message is driven home: a person staring at me, a stranger on a plane feeling compelled to buckle my seat belt, someone asking "what happened?" I am never allowed to forget that I don't have hands.

I am different in another way too—I am hyper-competitive. I will race you to the car, try to be the first one to unlock the door, and see if I can kick a ball farther than you. I can't tell you whether I come by my competitiveness naturally, or if it has been born of a desire to prove I can do things as well as anyone else, but it has shaped who I am. I didn't want to be called handicapped, I didn't want a handicapped parking pass, and I didn't want to compete in the Special Olympics. It's not that there is anything wrong with any of those things, but for me, I needed to ignore my problem and figure out ways to overcome my situation. If I was going to be the best, I wanted to be the best among *everyone*, without any conditions or caveats.

My parents had the same perspective. They decided early on that I would be treated like everyone else. They were determined that I would be "normal." In many ways, they fueled my competitiveness by allowing me (and even encouraging me) to see what I could do. If it was chore time, it was next man up on the list. They didn't know how I'd use a shovel, but they made me go out and pick up the dog crap in the yard if it was my turn. I was never allowed to use my handicap as an excuse—ever. We were expected to do things, and there was no getting out of it. From penmanship to sports to music, I was going to do it all, and I learned early on that there was no use trying to reason with either my mom or dad.

As I got older, the tasks became tougher. One day, I came home from high school and my mom met me with the news that the light bulb in the oven was out. The fact that it required a wrench and a screwdriver and was in an awkward position for anyone was irrelevant; it was my job to change it. It didn't matter that it would take me longer than my brothers to fix it or that there was a question about whether I could even reach it, the light had to be changed. And I had to do it. So, I figured it out.

I became good at figuring things out. Soon it was no longer about just figuring out a way to do the things that I needed to survive, it was about discovering what I *could* figure out. When I turned 16, it wasn't about learning to drive a car—that seemed too simple—I wanted to drive a manual transmission. And though I can't tie my shoes, I saw no reason why it should stop me from climbing a mountain, or belaying someone as they rappel off a cliff. It is an ability that has served me well throughout my life. I wasn't in search of an adrenaline rush; I just wanted to have a chance to do things "normal" people do, because in my mind, I was normal.

That desire to be normal extended into the things I wanted *not* to happen to me. I didn't want people to make a big deal out of my use of a fork, or to congratulate me for getting a Coke out of the vending machine. In my immature mind, these sorts of well-intentioned people were the enemy. It became my goal each day to make it through that 24-hour period without being made aware that I was handicapped. In that sense, most days were failures. As a result, my quest to fit in became even stronger. But the more I did to fit in, the more attention I would bring to myself. I wanted to be just one of the guys and play football, but each year some newspaper would "discover" that there was a no-handed linebacker and would write an article about me, further driving home the message that I was different. It was a self-perpetuating cycle.

I don't want to give the impression that this situation was an all-encompassing problem—like everything else, I figured out how to deal with it—and in reality I had a normal and happy childhood. I went to public school, played with my brothers and friends, and I joined in every activity possible. I learned how to listen to instructions or to watch an activity and immediately figure out how I could do it.

There were of course some spectacular failures, like the first time I tried fishing by myself. I drew the pole back and flung the line forward, just as I'd seen countless others do. Just like those countless others, my line flew out into the water, but unlike them, my pole and reel flew into the water with the line. I'm sure it still sits on the bottom of Lake Berryessa. But rather than becoming frustrated, I have come to look on those moments as opportunities to learn. Besides, rarely will I put myself in a position where I would look foolish in public. I will either figure it out on my own before I make an attempt, or I will work on it in the company of friends who will assist me when necessary, but who usually ignore my fits and starts (unless it's really funny, and then I'll never hear the end of it).

By the time I entered college, I came to the realization that perhaps I was the way I was for a reason. I would walk off the field after a college football game and a grown man would stop me and introduce his son or daughter. The first time it happened, I was clueless as to why this person would feel compelled to talk to me. I was always polite and would engage in some small talk, but it wasn't until they left and the dad would say, "I just wanted them to see you play" that I figured out why they'd bothered to talk to some small college linebacker. For some people, I was an inspiration. As a Christian, I had a deep belief that God had a plan for everyone, even kids with no hands, and soon, I was asked to speak at various youth groups about my life with a handicap. It was awkward for me at first, as I had spent most of my life trying to become invisible, but they seemed to relish the opportunity to hear the story about someone who had overcome an obstacle that had been put before them. The more I did of this, the more I realized I was helping people, and the more comfortable I became.

When I graduated from college, I was aware that having no hands was not a free pass. I had to find a job and make a living. So I looked for something I could do, confident that there was a career out there for an undersized linebacker who had spent his life creating a new definition for "manual dexterity."

Teaching and coaching interested me. Due to my time in front of those youth groups, I felt I would be good at it. Subsequently, after a semester of student teaching and coaching, I found out I was right. Still, it wasn't like anyone had explained to me how I might navigate a job interview given "my situation," and there were no classes in my teaching program that addressed the various ways to introduce my handicap to a class of 35. I finally came to the conclusion that teaching was like anything else—if you were confident and competent, people would trust you could do your job.

As a result, I would just ignore the fact that I held the chalk with two wrists and start teaching history. As long the students didn't ask, I wasn't going to tell. Eventually, like the kids who had been my friends in school, my students and colleagues figured out that it was a non-issue. And I had figured out that I was a teacher.

When I started as a teacher in California in the late 1970s, you had to do something extra if you were going to get the job. For me, it was a no-brainer—as someone who loved football and loved to teach, becoming a coach was a given. Early in my career, I became a head coach, and high school football coaches across the nation are always in demand as speakers for the local service clubs. Having finally gotten comfortable in front of an audience, I would routinely speak to them.

My talk would be about football, the team, and the importance of athletics. I would also tell a story or two about my life and dealing with my handicap. Each speech would lead to several more requests, and I quickly learned that I had a God-given talent for public-speaking. Being invisible was no longer an option. I was becoming older, wiser, and more mature, and I came to realize a very important truth: people are really hungry for a good story. And whether I believed it or not, my story was a good one.

My speaking career just kept growing. Though my primary job is currently as a head football coach (as it has been for a number of years), I have had the opportunity to speak to businesses, educators, students, and church groups across the country. Through my speeches and my travels, I have come to realize that my message about how I "figure it out" resonates with people everywhere.

The aforementioned brings me to the purpose of this preface. Why write a book? To me, it always seemed a little presumptuous to write a book about my life. On the other hand, after each speech, people would ask, "Do you have a book?" My answer was always no. On occasion, something funny, weird, or ridiculous would happen to me, and my fellow coaches would joke, "Hey, that should go in the book!" I must admit that I have had a unique and blessed life. Like many people, I fight the same battle everyday—mine just happens to include living without hands. Like many people, I know what it is like to be counted out, stereotyped, and discriminated against. Like many people, I know what it's like to fight, claw, and scratch for every gain. I have worked with many of these people in a quest to build a successful team, and my experiences have given me a deep appreciation about what is possible in life. It has also given me an appreciation for the human spirit and our ability to do more than we ever thought possible. While I have come to realize that success is defined at the level of the individual, I also believe that each of us has unlimited potential. We have the opportunity to redefine success every time we achieve it.

So, this is my story and why it has been written. It is my hope that you will find something of value within the following the pages, and I pray that it will be useful in your life.

Chapter 1 Tiny Tim

I don't think anyone will ever forget the birth of their first child, and I am no different. It was a sensory overload—the fluorescent lights reflecting off stainless steel, the metronomic beep of the heart monitor, the aroma of disinfectant, and the feel of a hospital mask every time I inhaled. I remember coaching my first wife, Melanie, through all of it—I reminded her of the breathing techniques we'd learned at Lamaze, I massaged every inch of her back and shoulders (twice), and I continually reminded her of how well she was doing. I didn't leave her side for a single bathroom break—only for a sandwich, when her labor seemed to stop progressing (take it from me future fathers—coaching can take a lot out of you). I was completely prepared and totally in the moment, which is all I ask for from my players, yet somehow, in the midst of it all, I saw an entire life flash before my eyes.

It was a kaleidoscope of family, friends, and football, sliced and diced by the hooks from which I'd liberated myself. There were awards and altars, monkey bars and Monterey Bay, and it was all thrown together into a piece of neurological abstract art. It was odd to look back on my life and not understand what I was seeing.

Then, I figured out what it was—my series of firsts. I saw my first day of school, walking up the steps knowing that if I had hands I wouldn't be there. I saw the first football game with my dad and getting the autographs of my favorite players. I saw the first concert my brother, Mike, and I played for the family, as the world's only banjo and trombone band. I saw my first day at one of California's first court-mandated integrated high schools and wondered for the first time if there might be someone who felt more out of place than me. I saw the first article about me in a newspaper sitting next to the first article about me in a tabloid. I also saw my first teaching job, and experienced my first interview, where I told my first (and only) lie about educational theorists.

And there I was in the hospital, in labor on Labor Day, about to add my first child to that list. I realized then that there's nothing more amazing, nothing more perfect than doing something for the first time. Now, I was about to become a first-time parent.

"It's a boy!"

I came out of my reminiscence and noticed that the doctor was cradling something in his arms.

"Mark, the cord?"

I gazed at the little writhing mass that was Tim Speckman.

"Mark." The breathless voice was Melanie's. "Go cut the cord."

"Oh." I felt Melanie release my arm and looked from Melanie's expectant face to the doctor's.

"Mark, come cut your son's umbilical cord."

I took a shaky step toward the now unmasked doctor. My eyes fixed on the pair of surgical scissors the nurse extended in my direction. They looked like the scissors our trainer used when he was taping up ankles, but it wasn't like I'd ever used them. Still, they had to be easier to work than a prosthetic hook, so I took them from her. I glanced down at the mass blood vessels and connective tissue that extended from my wife to my newborn son's mid-section. I let my eyes settle on Tim's little wrinkled face and smiled. I was about to cut my son free from his mother; I was officially bringing him into this world.

I manipulated the scissors until they were perfectly positioned and opened them. They flashed in the fluorescent light, and for a moment, I thought I was up on stage, 20 years later, demonstrating for awestruck German doctors again. *"Mark will now use the surgical scissors to cut through his son's umbilical cord. You will be able to ask questions after."*

I shook off the memory and snapped the scissors closed.

"Mark, I'd like to introduce you to Tim." The doctor stood and handed me my son.

I looked down at the little wonder I'd helped create. His face was scrunched into a tearless wail, and it made me wonder what it would be like to see his first smile. I felt him move his arm, and I noticed a bit of blood still clung to his little barrel chest. Balancing him on one arm, I carefully wiped it away.

"Well?"

I looked up at the sound of the nurse's voice.

"What do you think?"

"Alright," I traced one of Tim's fingers with my wrist, "he's got ten fingers, ten toes, and," I stole a glance to make sure, "one pecker."

My first son.

He was perfect.

Chapter 2 Look Ma, No Hands!

I was perfect when I was born.

That's what my mother said.

The doctor said the same.

They failed to mention one small thing to the infant that was passing between them.

I was born without hands.

Though I'm sure my wife, Sue, might validate this statement with other examples, I suppose there is more than a little truth to the axiom that no one is perfect.

The household I was born into, however, couldn't have been more perfect. My parents, Don and Jan Speckman, were the quintessential 1950s couple. My mother stayed home to tend to the large California house that my father paid for by working at a toy company. This scenario worked out perfectly for my older brother, Michael, who, when he wasn't playing with my father's company's next new product, acted as my mother's right hand. (To this day, she'll tell you that he'll do anything for her, as long as he isn't busy helping any of the other people that have come to rely on him.) It was as if I was becoming one of the Cleaver's—my father as Ward, my mother as June, and Michael as Wally. That would leave me as the Beaver, the one who created all of the chaos, set up all of the punch lines, and in the end, figured out the life lesson he was supposed to learn along the way. The only difference was, if Beaver had the help and support I had, it might have been the most boring show on television.

That support started from the moment I came into this world. Being born in 1955, my father wasn't in the room—no one besides the doctor, the nurse, and my mother were—and my mom wasn't even actively involved. The invention of "new" pregnancy drugs made it easier for women to give birth in every respect, and it was deemed better to do so in a stupor. My mother was comforted by the fact that her doctor looked like a doctor should look—tall, lean, and with a consistently thoughtful expression. As a result, when she came out of her induced slumber, she felt as if everything had gone just fine. That was when the doctor told her something was wrong. Still dazed, she could see my dad pacing next to her bed. The words that were coming out of the doctor's mouth weren't registering, though she was able to pick up that it was something about the appearance of my hands. In her mind, she determined that I must have some sort of birthmark.

The doctor informed my mother that I was a boy and this information excited her—she'd wanted another son. The doctor took advantage of my mother's bright outlook and began to "sell" me to her. He informed her that I had passed the Apgar test, signifying that I was capable of processing, that I was breathing perfectly, and that my heartbeat had a normal rhythm. He said the only thing that was abnormal was that I had been born without hands.

◆ ◆ ◆

It was at this point that my mother began to fully come around and notice that it was not just herself, her husband, and her doctor in the room. The grandparents were all milling about her bed, dressed up in their Sunday best and wailing as if they were at a funeral. When they saw that my mother was looking at each of them, tearful apologies came from every corner of the room and from underneath the brim of every grandmother's hat.

My mother was now pretty sure she knew what had happened, but she asked the doctor and nurse if she could see me. A look passed from one nurse to the other, and they tried to stall. It turned out that three days prior, a mother had tried to throw her baby out the window after discovering it had been born without feet. (That baby's condition was likely a by-product of another of the miracle 1950s fertility drugs, thalidomide. My mother did not, however, take this drug.)

Finally, at my mother's insistence, one of the nurses brought me to her. It was her turn to "sell" me. She took the long strands of hair I had growing on my head and curled them around her finger. She placed me on my mother's lap and told her with pride that I had all 10 toes. While she cradled me, my mom began to play with my feet, absentmindedly counting my digits. Each time she went through, she came up with the same number—nine. The nurse began to get worried, counted again, and apologized profusely for her mistake. She glanced nervously from my mother to the window and asked repeatedly if she could take me so my mom could rest. Without looking up, she thanked the nurse for her offer, accepted the apology, and asked rhetorically about my missing bit of anatomy, "What's a toe?"

◆ ◆ ◆

My father's mother, meanwhile, was bemoaning my "stumps" to anyone who would listen. (My mom still hates that word, preferring that my arms simply be called that; coincidentally, my former player and long-time racquetball adversary Eric Thomson will call me "Stumps" to throw me off my game.) My father, too, was becoming increasingly bothered by the absence of my hands. He became so agitated that, when everyone was informed by the nurse that it was time to give my mom some time to rest, rather than stay by her bed, he decided it would be best to drive out to his parent's house for dinner. This situation left my mother by herself with the prospect of raising a child with no hands.

With nothing other than an old issue of *Good Housekeeping* to entertain her (I had been taken to the nursery), my mother came upon an article that would change both her and my life. Its prose told the heart-wrenching tale of a child whose mother had died when he was young. This boy was adopted by the most ideal of families and had a life that most children would envy. But something was missing in this boy's life. He kept going to his dresser, opening each and every drawer, and breathing in the smell. Though the clothes weren't different, the odor was. It took him months to realize that his mother had placed soap in each and every drawer, ensuring a fresh scent when any was opened. The story left my mother in tears and with a newfound resolution: as long as I had a mother, my life was going to be just fine.

Chapter 3 Captain Hook

You wouldn't think, given the state of my arms, that my life would be changed by a trip to the country club, but it was. When I was 11 months old, my parents took me to my grandparents' country club to meet the friend of a friend who made prostheses. Robbie, the doctor, fit me for the newest in prosthetic technology, the wafer hook. The contraption was made out of plastic and rubber and was designed so that I had less of a chance of poking my eyes out. This possibility would have been a worry for my mom, even if I had only fingers attached to the end of my wrists.

It was breakfast when Robbie first installed my hooks, and I would imagine that, at eleven months old, I was hungry. Robbie had brought an extra set of the wafer hooks and he set about showing me how to hold a spoon. Once that had been accomplished, he demonstrated how to eat cereal. My mom says that within three viewings, I understood how to feed myself. From then on, I was on my own.

It wasn't always that easy raising a child with no hands. My mom will tell you that if it wasn't for my older brother, Michael, she doesn't know what she would have done with me. He would do anything, from getting me dressed in the morning to entertaining me, his hyperactive toddler brother. While Michael could act as a buffer between my mom and her household of boys, he couldn't insulate my mother from occasional comments she'd get from the rest of the family that reminded her son had been born without hands. Her father once suggested that "maybe Mark's hands will grow," as if fingers were something that came when Speckman's hit puberty.

Though I didn't get hands, at the age of five, I was upgraded from my wafer hooks to the more traditional metal ones. (I have always imagined that there must have been a transition period where they put little corks on the end to assuage any concerns that I might hurt someone with my prosthetic torture devices.) I was one of the first three children in the United States to be fit with these prostheses, and apparently among the first few in the world fit with hooks. I report this factor because it is from these that my earliest, most vivid memory of my childhood comes. I'm not talking about receiving the prosthetics from Robbie, but the demonstration I was asked to give before a panel of international doctors after I'd had them for two years.

Try to imagine being seven years old and being put on stage with a glaring spotlight obscuring your vision of the audience. Now, imagine that you are not Shirley Temple about to do a number with Al Jolson, but your average seven-year-old boy, with no hands and hooks that glinted when you moved them in the light. I don't know about you, but I just wanted to get out of there, to go home, and to play ball in the front yard with my brother. The doctors, however, had other ideas.

❖ ❖ ❖

"Mark."

"Yes?" I looked around the stage. It was empty except for me, the table with some toddler toys on it, and a Coke machine.

"Mark, would you take the square block and put it in the square hole?"

I peered out into the black void beyond the stage. It was impossible to see who was talking to me because of the brilliant white glow of the spotlight.

"Mark, would you please take the square block and put it in the square hole?"

Shrugging, I stepped behind the table, found the square block, grabbed it and dropped it through the hole.

In the audience, someone gasped. I could hear pencils scribbling in the front row.

"Mark, would you put the circular block in the circular hole?"

I picked up the circle and let it slide into the hole.

A low murmur drowned out the scratching of pens.

"Mark, would you put the triangle into the triangular hole?"

Was this what they brought me up to do? I had started the task before the questioner had finished speaking and completed it shortly thereafter.

"Mark, do you see the dime on the table?

I caught a glimpse of the shimmering coin and nodded at the light as if it was the one talking to me.

"Can you pick up the dime?"

With one of the hooks, I slid the dime to the edge of the table so nearly half of it was hanging off into space. With a flex of my left shoulder muscle, I opened my right hook and clamped it around the coin.

A couple of claps sounded from the audience of doctors—an applause cut off by professional propriety.

"Mark, can you put the dime into the Coke machine?"

I stepped over and dropped the coin into the slot. After several clunks, a bottle of soda dropped into the pan at the bottom of the machine.

"Can you open the bottle now Mark?"

With a shrug, I leaned down, grabbed the bottle with one hook and popped off the cap with the other.

"Can I have a drink?"

Stifled laughter filled the small auditorium.

"What?" the omniscient voice wavered. "Oh, yes, you can have a sip."

After my set was done, there was a question-and-answer period with the doctors who had observed me. Occasionally, I would field a question that was in English, but for the most part, they were in foreign languages. In some ways, this situation was more nerve-wracking than the performance on stage—with all of the different languages being thrown at me, I felt like the fates of all the world's handless children rested on my answers. As a seven-year-old, this sense quickly dissolved into frustration. The guttural inflections made it sound like I was getting scolded. Furthermore, it was the middle of summer—I just knew my family was out playing football without me. The questions they asked seemed really mundane as well—how did I pick up the block? How did I pick up the dime?—they were the type of questions seven-year-olds usually ask, not answer. Eventually, I was paroled and was able to play a little ball with my family before it was time to take the hour drive back home.

And so it was, yearly summer trips to Vallejo to get fitted for new hooks, to watch them bake in the heat of a kiln, while I baked in the heat of the sun, and, occasionally, to display my prosthetic prowess before a panel of adoring German doctors. All that work for some fake appendages that caused more trouble for me than they were ever worth.

Chapter 4 Not Your Average Show and Tell

Nursery school, apparently, was a cinch for me. My mom will tell you that not only was I allowed to do everything every other child did, but I would *do* everything every other child did. Stories, naps, art projects (I wish I had a videotape of the teacher asking the class to do a finger painting)—I did it all. Once, during the free-for-all that was parent pick-up time, an ambulance pulled up outside our classroom window. Seeing the flashing red lights, and the paramedics wheeling out a gurney, I knelt down to pray that no one was seriously hurt. My mom walked in as I was finishing the simple invocation and was moved to tears. She was certain then that sending me off to Catholic school the next year was going to be a perfect fit.

That wasn't the case.

◆ ◆ ◆

To say I was prepared for first grade was an understatement. In addition to my time at nursery school, my mom and Michael kept me in a constant academic and social double team.

Could I write my name?

Check.

Could I open and close my backpack?

Check.

Could I recite my address and phone number?

Check.

Could I tie my shoes?

No check.

Michael would have to help me with that in the morning before school.

Still, I was ready when the first day of school came. I had new clothes, new shoes, and a new backpack, filled with a lunch for me and a lunch my mother had made for the nuns. The school just wasn't ready for me.

As I alluded to previously, birth defects were not an uncommon occurrence in the mid-50s, and it should have been no surprise that there was a handicapped child already enrolled at the school. I don't know if that other kid was a handful or if someone doubted my self-sufficiency, but the church determined that they could not handle anyone else with what they considered a disability. This came as a shock to my mother, who rattled off a list of things I could do without hands that would have kept me in front of the German doctors for days. She reminded them that my father's sister was a Sister in the church, but it was to no avail. My father went higher up the chain and confronted the priest, who, though very embarrassed, explained that there was nothing he could (or wanted to) do.

So, my parents did what they had to—they pulled Michael out of the private school and traipsed us over to the public one to see if they would have a problem with me being enrolled there. The principal gave my mother a tour of the building and informed her that it would be fine with him if I was to attend his school. (That would suggest that it might have been less than fine—amazing how attitudes have changed since then.) And so began my official education—and a life that would be reset every fall and punctuated by winter, spring, and summer breaks.

That education would begin with the old curmudgeon, Mrs. Anderson, whom my mother had informed, was to treat me like everyone else. This attitude was great in the classroom. I found addition easy (especially when food was involved) and subtraction hard. I was able to outpace some classmates as we would copy countless sentences from the board. In fact, my hand(less) writing was even used as a model for the other students. Strangely enough, it was during PE and recess that I had the most difficulty. It wasn't that the teacher thought I wouldn't be able to participate—it was that she thought I should do *everything*. We would run—I'd be great. Soccer—I can't tell you how many goals I scored. Basketball—I wasn't much of a scorer, but I ruled the boards (though in my stat line next to rebounds you might find the new category "popped balls" with an eerily similar number). Four square—terrific, until you asked someone to remove the deflated ball from my hook.

As was (and based on Tim's education still is) typical of elementary school, we had a square dancing unit that winter. I knew that there was nothing I would be able to pop, but I still wasn't sure I wanted to participate because of the cootie factor. That apprehension was probably heightened in the minds of the girls who would have to deal with my "hook cooties."

In spite of both sides' consternation about my status as a dancer, Mrs. Anderson came to the conclusion that I was going to be a participant. (I still don't know if that decision was made because she was oblivious of other students' disdain for my hardware or some research she'd done that definitively proved that cooties could not survive for any length of time on stainless steel.) Overcoming these psychological obstacles became impossible when every other command was "take your partner's hand."

So, having learned nothing from her experiences in our other class periods, Mrs. Anderson asked if I would be willing to be in charge of keeping the tambourine to the beat of the music. Certain what I was doing was important, I focused on hitting the instrument with just enough force to get the requisite jangle but not enough to punch a hole through it. That worked great in the slow songs, but the moment a song with a real beat came on, I got a little too fired up and…well, you can guess what happened.

The greatest debacle, however, was the day Mrs. Anderson decided that we were going to tackle the monkey bars. The day's program didn't need much in the way of introduction, considering the fact that recess had been going for weeks, and some of my classmates had taken it upon themselves to become certifiable simians, capable going across forwards, backwards, and doing flips. I didn't really run with that crowd. So, as I stood in line waiting for my turn, I fidgeted with the zipper on my coat, nervous about what I would do when I was up. In every other activity, even those where I might perpetrate equipment homicide, I was certain I was going to figure out a way to participate. But this piece of equipment, named after another animal with opposable thumbs, seemed beyond the limits of my ability.

"Mark, it's your turn."

I looked up from my zipper at Mrs. Anderson. "I, I don't know if I can do this."

"Mark," the teacher fixed me with a glare, "your mother told me on the first day of school that you were to do everything the other students did."

"I…" The words got caught in my mouth.

"Go on. The other kids are waiting."

I looked up at the iron cross bar that seemed to span a psychological precipice. I took a deep breath and stepped up to the top wrung of the entry ladder. I hoisted my left arm above my head and for the first time, I felt the weight of my hooks.

TING!

My hook rattled as I cupped it over the first bar. I refused to look back over my shoulder, but I could hear the other kids talking and laughing behind me. Were they talking and laughing about me? I swallowed hard and extended my right arm up to the bar. It felt heavier than my left.

TING!

The second hook was in position. I closed my eyes. It was time for me to make my leap of faith.

Catholic though I was, the laws of gravity prevailed on that day.

My feet plummeted toward the ground before the tension in my hooks' rubber bands slowed me to a stop. My arms of my jacket, stretched to the limit, kept my prosthetics and the harness together, though it must have looked like my arms themselves had become detached from my body.

I looked up at Mrs. Anderson, expecting that she would have a solution.

A look of abject terror flashed across her face.

"Run!"

The word had come from the mouth of my teacher. She rushed past me with her arms spread, presumably to herd the students into the building, though I can't be sure—although I was twisting a bit, it was never enough to capture a glance of what was happening behind me. The moment I heard the outside door slam though, I knew I was completely alone.

I can't tell you what a six-year-old thinks about when he is dangling from the monkey bars by near prototype prosthetics because I honestly don't remember. Were this to happen to me today, I might have said, "I told you so," or, "On your way back to the classroom, can you pick up a patent application—I think I just invented bungee jumping."

Luckily, I didn't have a long time to think.

The school intercom crackled to life.

"Would Michael Speckman please report to the playground? Michael Speckman, please report to the playground."

As if he were an industrial worker being called to the office to take an urgent telephone call, my brother was being summoned to save me.

Within a couple of minutes, Michael was next to me, breathing hard from his run across the asphalt, using his third-grade mind to intuit a way to get me down. After several failed attempts to lift me up so that I could reconnect with the rest of my arms and then lift myself clear of the bars, Michael simply pushed me back to where I'd started, climbed up behind me, and pulled my hooks free. After that was finished, there was nothing else to do. We went back to class, Michael without his breath, me without functional rubber bands.

I don't know that I consciously thought it, but I believe that subconsciously, that was the beginning of the end for my hooks.

Chapter 5 The Great Equalizer

My arms were the least of my worries; at least that's what the doctors all seemed to think. They all seemed to be more interested in my eyes and my feet. Having been born cross-eyed, by the time I was five, I'd already had five surgeries on my eyes to "straighten" them. (Though finally corrected, there are still times when, after looking at film for 10 hours, my right eye will slip back into its original conformation.) My feet, however, were a source of intrigue to the doctors well into high school.

Few of the podiatrists had seen anyone born with one foot that was a full size smaller than the other, and none had seen anyone born without a big toe. They wanted to know everything—did it hurt when I stood? Walked? How about when I ran?—and they put me through every test they could think of (e.g., X-rays, filming my movements). This assessment was done to both help me with the pain I felt when I ran and to satisfy their own scientific curiosity. The deal seemed to work out for both parties—they got to poke, prod, and probe my feet every year, and I got orthotics that made it so I could do what I really wanted: play sports.

My dad, on the other hand, didn't do anything to help me play sports—other than provide me with opportunities to play. It was ingenious. He never went outside with me and said, "Well, let's see if we can figure out how to help Mark catch the football." It was just, "Michael, Mark, you want to go outside and play ball?" Then, we'd go out and play.

I'm not going to say that I wasn't at a disadvantage, because I was, but then so is every other younger brother. When you are younger, you have to fight for every opportunity and take advantage when one comes. New York Giants quarterback Eli Manning has said in interviews that he was always a center when his brothers, Peyton (Indianapolis Colts quarterback) and Cooper, and his father, Archie (New Orleans Saints quarterback), would go out and play football. Every now and then, he would be allowed to go deep. If he caught it, his brothers trumpeted their congratulations. If he dropped it, he wouldn't see the ball the rest of the day. It was no different for me—I just needed to figure out how to catch the bomb.

Learning how to catch the football was the easy part. Without my hooks and with the dexterity I had in my wrists, I could snatch any pass Michael would throw me. But, I wanted to play quarterback. So, I set about teaching myself how to throw a spiral with two wrists instead of one hand. By the time I was done, even though I couldn't throw quite as far as some of my friends, I was at least as accurate as they were.

It didn't stop there. At that time, I was too young to play organized football, but there were 10-year-old basketball leagues, and there was basketball at recess. At recess, teams would be picked by two captains, and because of the reputation I'd earned earlier in life as a "ball-popper," I wasn't often chosen to play. The recreational league teams, however, had to play me. Because games were on the weekends, I knew I would be able to play them without my hooks, whereas at school trying to take them off and put them back on during a recess period was prohibitive.

Having no hooks meant that there was no way anyone would be able to blame me for any popped balls or be intimidated by my racing down-court with a pair of steel scythes. We were all going to be wearing the same uniforms, shooting at the same hoop, and playing under the same rules. We were all equals. Whoever was the best would play the most. So, I started to work my butt off. I practiced lay-ups, jumpers, and bank-shots on the hoop in our driveway. I didn't tell anyone about what I was doing, and I only worked out when I was sure no one was watching. I was going to shock the world come game time.

Sports, at their essence, are a true meritocracy, and that is what Ronald Reagan loved about them. I love that too. There is extraordinary satisfaction that comes when you see preparation validate itself with victory. And it happened that, in our first game of the year, my preparation was going to be tested. We were playing in front of what felt like a huge crowd (maybe 75 people), and the game went down to the wire. We were down one with 10 seconds left, and our guard who was capable of dribbling with either his right or his left hand (a rarity among 10-year-olds) brought the ball up the court. As is common in youth basketball, one of the defenders left his man to run at the guy with the ball. The vacated player happened to be me. Our point guard, seeing this impromptu double-team, threw me the ball. I caught it 12 feet from the basket. Without a second thought, I turned, jumped, and fired off a jump shot.

SWISH.

The crowd erupted. The shock and elation on everyone's face was as if I had somehow managed to place a man on the moon—with no hands (imagine how the German doctors would have reacted to that). I should have been ecstatic too, and I was…but I wasn't. I was happy that I'd hit the shot that got our team the victory, but I wasn't amazed. That was why I'd been shooting in the driveway at all odd hours of the morning and night. I was simply the guy who did his job when his team needed him. No congratulations were necessary.

◆◆◆

By the end of that season, I was feeling pretty good about myself. Good enough to take on the last of the big three sports—baseball.

One day, while Mike and I were sitting on the floor in our room, the opportunity presented itself.

"You want to go play catch?"

I looked around the room for some sort of ball. "With what?"

"With this." Mike tossed a leather glove my way.

I cradled my arms and caught it against my chest.

Without another word, we jogged out to the front yard and set up about 30 feet apart.

"Aren't you going to put on the glove?"

I looked down at the mitt I was still swaddling like an infant. There were five finger holes but no room for a wrist. Still, I wedged the glove against my mid-section and crammed my left wrist as far into the middle of the mitt as I could. I held up my arm in what I was pretty sure was the universal baseball signal for "throw it."

Mike hurled the ball. It was headed just outside my left shoulder. I adjusted the glove's position and waited for impact.

POP!

The glove closed perfectly around the ball.

Then, it hit the ground two feet behind me.

I looked up at Mike. He was fighting off laughter.

Grumbling, I pulled the ball out of the mitt and threw it back with both arms. I picked up the mitt, shoved it back on with all of my might, and turned back to Mike with my left arm raised.

With a shrug, he threw it again.

The same result.

I ground my teeth and threw the ball back again. This wasn't catch—it was fetch with a mitt.

I looked down at the mitt I was cradling in my arms and smiled at my brother. "Go ahead, throw it."

Mike looked at me like I was crazy. "You're sure?"

"Throw it."

The smile on his face disappeared, and he tossed the ball toward me.

I positioned myself directly in front of the ball.

THUD.

I watched as the ball bounced off my 10-year-old chest and into my awaiting glove.

"Ooooh." Mike grimaced. "Did that hurt?"

I looked down at the ball nestled in the web of the glove. A perfect catch. "Nope."

"Wow. That was like a bank shot."

"Yep." I set the glove down, extracted the ball, and threw it back.

Mike shot me a quizzical look. "You want to do it again?"

I picked the mitt back up and prepared to resume my role as baseball backboard.

"Okay."

We played catch for probably no more than 10 minutes, before we decided to do something else. By the time we went in for dinner, I was starting to feel a little sore, but I really didn't think anything of it—I'd already learned that sports can make you hurt a little bit. Because it was hot that day, my shirt was pretty sweat-soaked, and my mom told me to take off my shirt and put it into the washing machine.

She stopped me before I could make it two steps.

"Mark! What happened to you?"

I looked down at my chest. It was covered with circles of various sizes and colors.

"What are we talking about?" My father had just gotten home from work and saw us standing in the kitchen.

"Well—"

"Did somebody tie you up and throw rocks at you?"

"No, Mike and I were just playing catch with a baseball."

Mike came over to get a look at my chest. "Those must be the seams of the ball." He pointed at one of the redder marks on my chest.

"Are you trying to kill yourself?" My father shook his head. "No more catch with the baseball for you—you need to stick to basketball."

"But—"

"No 'buts.' Now, go to your room and get ready for dinner."

I think my father, mother, and Mike all thought that was the end of it.

But it wasn't.

That night I lay in bed thinking about what my dad had said. My parents had never stopped me from doing anything because I didn't have hands—I took out the trash, I raked the leaves, I did all my homework—but now they were going to keep me from playing my brother's favorite sport? If they wanted to tell me I couldn't clean up the dog poop because I didn't have hands, great, but I was not going to be denied America's pastime. Still, my attempt to play catch that afternoon had been an utter failure (unless you call the ground catching both the ball and the mitt success). I needed a new technique, and I stayed up all night devising and rejecting plans for playing catch the next day.

By the next morning, I had an idea I thought would work.

That afternoon, I put the plan in action.

"Hey Mike, you want to go out and play catch?"

"With what?"

I smiled and tossed him the baseball.

"No way. You heard what dad said. If he finds out, he's going to kill you."

"Oh, come on Mike. He won't find out unless you tell him."

Mike eyed the baseball, the mitts, and me. "Okay, grab your mitt. But, you better yell if you even hear a car a block away—I'm not going to get in trouble for this."

We ran outside and set up the same way we had the day before, Mike on one end of the yard, me on the other.

"Okay Mike—throw it."

"What are you doing? You've got two—"

"Just shut up and throw it!"

Mike rolled his eyes and tossed the ball to me. The throw was a bit off line, but I side-stepped in front of it and, with one wrist wedged into the thumb hole of the mitt and one stuffed as far into the pinky as it would go, I centered the glove on the hurtling ball.

SNAP.

The glove closed itself around the ball. There had been no impact with my chest and no running after the ball and mitt. Both remained firmly in my possession.

"Nice catch." Mike nodded his approval, but a smirk was on his face. "Now how are you going to throw it back?"

I glared at my brother as I set the glove down, pulled out the ball, and fired it back at his chest. "Like that."

Mike smiled. "That'll work."

Granted, I wasn't going to be turning two for the Yankees, but nobody was going to tell me I couldn't figure out a way to play baseball.

Chapter 6 The Word Is "*Hand*icapped," Not "*Hook*icapped"

The thing teenagers want, more than anything else, is to be accepted for who they are. They don't want to be seen as weird, odd, or different. That's why they surround themselves with peers of similar interests, looks, and desires. It means they are a part of something bigger than them. It means they belong. Coincidentally, that is the same thing handicapped people want, only they will do it in hopes of disappearing into the crowd. So, by the time I was a teenager, being the kid with the type of shiny hooks that have made their way into the lexicon of campfire stories made it more than a little difficult to fit in. I had grown to hate my hooks, and it was time to be rid of them.

Though I'd had success at things like basketball without my prosthetics, for the most part, I still wore them every time I went out in public, all the way through elementary school. I'd become pretty good with them, having taught myself to throw a pencil up with one arm and catch it in the other, and my aunt used my abilities to punish those who had doubted me. Being a sister in the church that had denied me access to their school, she was able to ordain me as an altar boy. That way, she could parade me in front of the priest every week, having me light candles and carry out sacraments before an adoring audience.

I don't know if the fact that I was given an award for catechism served as a vindication for the priest or was a further chastisement of his and the school's decision, but it was certainly something that seemed to make my aunt and mother happy. As for me, I could have cared less. I didn't want to be known as "the cute altar boy with no hands"—I wasn't even sure I wanted the attention that came from being an altar boy. I just wanted to be known as Mark. And the first time that really happened was on the football field.

❖ ❖ ❖

Sixth grade was the earliest you could sign up for football, and I wasn't surprised when my dad made sure that I was among the first in line. While this step ensured I *had* a place on the team, it didn't determine *what* my place on the team would be. The first decision that had to be made was what I was going to do with my hooks. Since there were going to be more people out there, both playing and watching, my mom came to the conclusion that I should be wearing my prosthetics. The coaches, in all of their infinite wisdom, came to the conclusion that the hooks would be okay so long as there was a sock over the top of them.

In order to fully cover the prosthesis, it would have to be a tube sock, which barely had enough cushioning for my mangled feet, much less a perfectly curved piece of stainless steel. I remember thinking that it was a bad idea—I was worried about hurting the other kids and about getting hurt myself. The prosthetics didn't feel good when they were yanked odd directions. When I explained this situation to my mother, she was sympathetic, and when I informed my father I couldn't catch or throw with my hooks on, I never had to wear them to play football again. I'd won that battle.

I also won the battle over how I should ride my bike. Nobody wore helmets in those days. But because most people could grip the handlebars, parents were left with the reasonable notion that their kids were at least in control of their own destiny. At that point, it just would come down to how much common sense you had imparted to them.

My parents, on the other hand, must have been mortified. *What if Mark hits a bump and flies off the bike? Should Mark have foot brakes when he can't hold the handlebars, or hand brakes when he has no hands to grab them with?* The questions were existential in a sense, for they were going to show as much about what kind of parents they were going to be as they were going to show about what kind of bicyclist I was going to be. But they never showed any hesitation; they just put me on Mike's old bike. They must have come to the conclusion that being able to feel the handlebars was more important than being able to grip them. As a result, I was taught to ride without my hooks. I adapted (by learning to watch where I was going), and they adapted (by not overanalyzing my actions). In time, my friends and I rode all over the neighborhood.

In fact, about the only thing that could slow me down was my hooks. They were heavy, awkward, and designed by people with hands. Inventors seemed to try to get inside the head of people like me when creating devices to help, but I always thought their audience was more like people who had lost their hands in an accident or in a war. These were people whose brains were wired for digits—mine wasn't. But I was too young to realize or articulate these thoughts, and since my parents thought the hooks were the best solution money could buy, I wore them like I was told.

Until I was out of their sight.

By the time I was in middle school, I figured out that, so long as I had my hooks on when I got on the bus and when I got off, my parents would assume I had not gone to the trouble of removing them. (There were bands and cords and a harness and all of it had to be tightened and balanced, and it was near impossible to try to do all of it by myself.) Luckily, my friends or my brother would help me take them off and put them on.

This situation was great on a couple of levels. For one, it expedited the process. But more importantly, it became an excuse for my friends and I to milk our lunch breaks. My friend would explain to our teacher that I needed help putting back on my hooks (while I feigned being too prideful to ask). We would, of course, be granted permission to take any extra time we needed, which usually amounted to no more than five minutes. On rare occasions, however, it could be stretched out to 10. The thing was, I really didn't want to wear my hooks for class—especially during band. And, it was band that I had after lunch.

❖ ❖ ❖

I can see that, when I tell people I used to play in the school band, they assume it was an honorary position given to a person with a unique proclivity for the triangle. But no, I was in band because I had a trombone. Only, I didn't have it because of some deep-seeded passion I had for music or because I wanted to see if I could figure out how to play an instrument—I had a trombone because of the Kennedys.

Our family was modeled after the Kennedys. My mother loved the Kennedys. She figured that with a family of three boys and one girl, we could be just like their family of three boys and one girl. (In reality, I've always thought we were closer to the Osbournes.) In one of the countless profiles written about them, my mom discovered that each of their four children played a musical instrument. As a result, we were going to learn to play instruments.

Michael, being the oldest, was the first to get his instrument. At the time (or any time really), there was no instrument that was cooler than the guitar, and he wanted one. Though we were never especially well off, our grandparents were, and between my mom's insistence that we become musicians and my brother's desire to own a guitar, he was feeling pretty good about Christmas that year. He was feeling even better when we woke up Christmas morning and found a huge box with his name on it. I'm sure he could already hear the riffs coming from the Gibson® guitar that was hidden beneath that wrapping paper.

Only it wasn't a guitar.

It was a banjo.

I remember laughing when my brother hotly held up the least cool instrument in the strings family. As my laughter was just beginning to dissolve into giggles, Mike read the second part of his present: he had been given six weeks of banjo lessons. I just about died. (To this day, when Mike takes out his banjo or his mandolin, I can't help but think about the one stringed instrument he still can't play—the guitar.)

I don't know if it is hubris or ignorance that led me to believe that my mother—the one who told every teacher I'd ever had to treat me like every other student—was going to give me a free pass, but I was certain there was going to be no surprises on the instrument-front for me. Would Jackie have ever done anything for Jack that she wouldn't have done for Bobby? No. Then, Jan wasn't going to do anything for Mike that she didn't do for Mark.

So, when we were out school shopping before I began seventh grade, my mom led me into a music store. I figured it was a break from the intensive shirts, shoes, and supplies shopping we'd been engaged in, and I allowed myself to gaze about at the glistening instruments. As I was eyeing a polished Les Paul guitar, I felt my mother's long fingers close around my elbow and thrust my arm into the air.

"Excuse me?"

It was my mother's voice, but there was no one in our vicinity to whom she could be talking. I double-checked to see if it was me, but I saw that she was looking toward the back of the store.

"Excuse me?"

I used my mom's gaze as a guide and saw that she was looking at the person standing behind the counter.

The two sets of eyes must have been enough to get the guy's attention, because he shouted back at us.

"Yes? Can I help you?"

"Well sir, I was wondering, what kind of instrument can he play?"

I whipped my head around to look at my mom. She was pointing at my hooks.

"Well..." The man picked at a pimple on the side of his face and looked around the store.

"Mom? What are you doing?" I pulled my arm free and glared at her.

She continued to look at the 18-year-old clerk, as if he was the head conservator at Julliard.

"I guess he could play..." the man's eyes seemed to settle on some object hung on a distant wall, "the drum."

He looked at me. I don't recall saying anything, but the look on my face must have suggested that he should come up with another option. I didn't want to be the poor guy in the parade who just pounded away at the big drum—could I at least play the drums?

"Or, he could play the trombone."

The two options seemed to satisfy my mom. "Well Mark, which will it be?"

Though it was a no-brainer, I hesitated, hoping that she would remember that this was just an elaborate joke that she'd decided to play on me. When she continued to wait, I simply said "trombone."

◆ ◆ ◆

Picking the trombone for me was absolutely ingenious (perhaps that clerk did one day end up at Julliard). It had no strings and no buttons, with only a spit valve and the end of the slide that were a bit tricky for me to work. All I had to do was move the slide to one of seven positions. But that didn't mean it was easy.

From the first day I got that trombone, I knew how Michael felt on Christmas. And just like him, I wasn't laughing—I was complaining.

Mom, can I quit?

No, we have a three-month lease.

Can I pay you for it?

You don't have any money. Now, go practice.

Going to practice did not mean go see if I could play the piece my teacher gave me, or even work my way through the scales; it meant see if I could get a note out. For days, I would blow on that trombone. The only thing that came from it were sounds that would make a whoopee cushion proud. One day my dad had enough.

"God Mark, you sound awful." He shooed me off my chair in the living room and picked up my music stand. "Follow me."

I trailed him with my curled piece of brass (when I held it, it didn't deserve to be called an instrument), until we stopped in the garage.

He deposited my stand in front of the Rambler station wagon. "You can sit on the hood and practice out here."

Without another word, he left me in the garage, with my trombone, my music, and the dog. Two "notes" later, the dog left.

Life was no better at school. The kid with no hands was carrying the biggest instrument case on the school bus. Don't think I didn't stand out in a crowd.

The worst times with the instrument for me, however, were in band class. It was there that I got the opportunity to prove to the world that my dad wasn't just being a jerk for putting me out in the garage. When everyone was playing, I was fine; I could hide my wretchedness behind those of the trumpets, French horns, and the clarinets. But, when that band teacher would ask for the trombones to play measures 12 through 18 again, all eyes were on me. The ones I remember most are those of the little girls with flutes. At that moment, to me, being a flautist was worse that being racist, sexist, Marxist—every kind of "ist" there was. They would giggle, whisper, and roll their eyes (sometimes all at once) when I screwed up. I wanted to throw my trombone at the band teacher and storm out of the class.

Then, one day, I played it right.

The girls smiled at me.

I liked playing the trombone.

✦ ✦ ✦

As with everything else (besides sports), I wore my hooks when I played in public. My mother's argument in favor of the ceramic and steel appendages seemed bolstered by the fact that the only way I could reach the seventh position was when I was wearing my prosthetics. Even then, however, it was a stretch. It wasn't as if the hooks provided much tactile sensation (in reality, they provided none), but at least in close proximity to my body, I could *imagine* I was feeling what I was doing. At a distance, it was a whole different matter, and seventh position was nothing if not at a distance.

So, there we were in May, poised before a crowd of adoring parents, grandparents, friends, and acquaintances, about to give our biggest performance of the year. (There was always more buzz about these middle-school performances than there should have been, but our band teachers were quite esteemed, and the community anticipated these events with great fervor.) I was decked out in my finest clothes, short of my altar boy outfit, and I had taken my position near the back of the risers. I could see the capacity crowd, and, as a person driven by competition, I was more excited to be playing an instrument than I thought was possible.

When the performance began, I was on fire. Every note was pitch perfect and on time. The slide felt like it belonged in my hook, and the freshly oiled brass seemed to glide as if gravity and friction didn't exist.

And, when I went for seventh position, they apparently didn't.

It was the crescendo of the piece, and as I thrust the slide out toward it's limit, the brass grip slid from my hook's grasp. The momentum of the piece of metal carried it free of its position as a part of my instrument.

The slide was flying.

THUNK!

THUNK!

THUNK!

The piece of the instrument had managed to elude all of the other players, striking only the carpeted risers on the way down to the floor.

By the look on his face, my teacher, Mr. Nelson, had noticed the disparate chord of my rogue piece of instrumentation. Conductor Nelson continued to sweep his baton, ensuring the piece could begin to mellow appropriately. Leaning over, Maestro Nelson picked my slide off the bottom step of the risers, stepped between two confused flautists, and slipped it back into its housing with a wink.

No wonder the public appreciated him. At that moment, I did too.

❖ ❖ ❖

Teachers weren't always able to help me avoid embarrassment. I remember being 13 and standing in line at See's Candies®. As always happened when I was out in public, it was an observant little kid with a big mouth who first noted my absence of hands. This situation still happens, and whenever convenient, I will avoid walking directly into the sightline of what I imagine to be precocious pre-teens.)

"Mom," the kid pulled on his mother's jacket, "mom, look at that boy!"

The exasperated mother looked up and caught a glimpse of my hooks. Her eyes widened. She whipped her head around toward her son and held her hand to her lips.

"But mom," the child cocked his head, unsure if his mother had seen what he was talking about, "that boy has no—"

"You be quiet." Her whisper was loud enough to be heard over the din in the store.

The kid turned from his mother back to me.

Embracing my role as the freak in this little family drama, I slowly raised one of my hooks and twisted it about in front of my face. I opened the hook and pretended to examine its curves—then snapped it shut with an audible "click."

The kid's jaw dropped, but not before a gasped "Mom" escaped his lips.

"Quiet!"

I could tell the mom was pretending not to notice that half of the eyes on the store were on her (the other half was trying not to be on me). Skillfully waiting until the boy's eyes wandered back my way, I locked the boy in a stare and affected as deranged a look as I could muster.

"Mom!"

"That's enough!" The woman grabbed her son by the shoulder of his coat and half-dragged him out of the store.

It was funny at the time. Now, I'm afraid some poor soul is running around the country with an irrational fear of amputees.

Sometimes, I didn't have to work so hard to get people's goats—I was able to disarm them with their own words. I recall in my early teens taking our family dogs for a walk and sitting down on a grassy knoll at the park. I had the dogs' leashes in my hooks and my hooks stuck in my pockets. Because it was a bit chilly that day, I was wearing a coat. Our dogs were young and cute, making them the proverbial kid magnet. Inevitably, a five-year-old wandered up to me.

"Are your dogs nice?"

"Nice?" I asked.

"Do they bite?" The child was already reaching for one of the dogs.

I shook my head. "Look what they did to me." I took my arms out of my pockets.

The kid pulled his arm away. His face flushed, and he took off screaming for his mother.

Unfortunately, opportunities like that were few and far between. Mostly, my hooks were a pain in the ass.

When it came time for that ultimate in teenage rites of passage, I let it be known that I wanted to go through it sans hooks. But, like everything else, because a driving test was to be taken in public, my parents made sure I was wearing my hooks.

That lasted until I bounced the car onto the curb pulling up to the DMV. At that point, I declared to my mom that I was not going to be taking this test wearing hooks. There, just outside where I was going to be evaluated and in front of the world, I took off my shirt, removed my prosthetics, and threw them in the back seat. I was going to take this test not being able to *hold* the steering wheel and stick shift, but *feel* them.

I passed.

It was then that I realized that my life to that point had been about holding on. Both my family and I had been holding on to a semblance of normalcy and holding on to the safety bar of prosthetics, designed by people with hands. Life in general—not to mention life without hands—was too complicated to worry about how I was going to get a grip on it. As a blind man scaling a rock face would tell you, a hand-hold may keep you secure, but it won't get you anywhere. You've got to feel your way to a different point in order to make it to the top. As such, I was determined to feel my way through the rest of my life.

It was shortly after that test that I was sitting in Robby's office, looking across the desk at not only Robby but both of my parents.

"Think of your prosthetics like a shovel," Robby explained, "they're a tool to be used."

"But, a tool is supposed to help you," I shot back.

"You need the hooks to write," my dad said.

"I write better without them."

"What about the trombone?" my mom asked.

"I play it better without them."

We continued like this through countless mundane tasks.

"Is there anything you can do with the hooks that you can't without?" Robby asked.

I had to think about that. "Yes."

Robby leaned forward in his chair. My parents inched closer to me.

"With my hooks, I can hold a pencil in one arm and a glass of water in the other."

Robby nodded, and my parents exchanged knowing glances.

"But, in order to do that I have to close my hooks so one of them is in the glass. That makes it awkward and nasty to drink, and I can't write especially well with my hook. I would be faster just setting the pencil down, taking a drink, and then going back to writing." I shrugged. "Besides, who tries to write and drink at the same time? It would be a neat trick if someone could."

No one responded. It seemed that we were at an impasse. And, as someone who has survived parenting three teenagers, I can tell you that is the same as a victory for the teenager.

I had figured out how to outwit my parents.

I wouldn't be wearing my hooks anymore.

Chapter 7 Remember the ~~Titans~~ Mighty Scots

When the movie *Remember the Titans* was released, it brought back a lot of memories. As a football coach, I could relate to the travails of attempting to get both players and coaches to subjugate their egos and embrace their roles on a team. Furthermore, as someone who grew up in the 60s, I could relate to the racial turmoil depicted in the film. I'm sure there are countless people who fall into both categories for whom this film held meaning (not to mention the fact that it just makes for enjoyable viewing). But, that wasn't really what struck me about the movie. What struck me was the fact that I attended one of the schools that was, by government mandate, integrated. It felt to me, when I watched "Remember the Titans" for the first time, that I was reliving my childhood.

The rumors started my eighth-grade year. "Blacks" were going to be attending Carlmont High School the next year with us. I thought this story was ridiculous—there were no black people to be found in Belmont or San Carlos ("Carlmont" got its name by combining the names of the two cities). I didn't see them at school, I didn't see them at the mall; the only time we ever saw black people was when we tripped into the city (San Francisco). San Francisco had people who represented every facet of the color spectrum. The rumors persisted all summer, and I was curious, come the first day of school, whether they were going to prove false or not.

Carlmont, like many high schools, had a long drive before the front entrance, where parents and buses would drop their students off. I remember standing there before school on that first day and seeing a fleet of yellow buses pull in together. I'd never known buses to pull in as a giant convoy, and I watched with curiosity as lines of black students began descending the stairs of the vehicles. That curiosity turned to shock when I realized there were nearly 500 students of a different ethnicity than the rest of Carlmont, mulling about the front walk. It felt as if the buses had come from another planet. And, even though they had just come from East Palo Alto, that 15-minute drive must have felt like a shuttle trip to the moon for them.

By that point, football had already started, but for most of the kids from East Palo, Alto the first day of school was the first day of practice. You would have thought tensions would be high (and they might have been on the varsity squad), but the moment we put our shoulder pads and helmets on, everybody was trying to block and tackle everyone else. After a day of losing sweat and gaining bruises, we figured out that it didn't matter if you were white or black, football was still football, and jokes about what happened on and off the field were funny, no matter who you were.

This frame of mind was not the case for the rest of the school. Tension was felt by everyone, and the chosen method for alleviating that tension my freshman and sophomore years was name-calling. By my junior year, this situation had escalated to fights, and in my senior year, a brawl broke out. The National Guard and a SWAT team appeared, toting guns, masks, and canisters of tear gas. The principal made the decision to shut down the school for the day, and the officers bluntly conveyed that message.

"Get the hell out!"

✦ ✦ ✦

When we came back to school, I wrote an editorial that was published in our school's newspaper, explaining why shutting the school was the right thing to do. My buddy wrote an opposing editorial, espousing the point of view that what the administration had done was wrong. Regardless of our (or any other students') sentiments, the administration knew that something needed to be done. One of their decisions was to extend a metaphorical olive branch to the black students.

As a result, as a part of the yearbook awards section, several new categories were created, including "Best Afro," "Best Dancer," and "Done Most for Black Student Union." These awards were essentially earmarked for my black classmates, and I thought it was great that they were going to receive the kind of positive recognition that had been largely denied them during their time at Carlmont. (That didn't mean that I didn't feel a bit gypped when I didn't win "Best Afro".) In addition to simply recognizing that Carlmont had multiple cultures, the administration's second step was an overt attempt to integrate those cultures into a single cohesive student body—or at least one that didn't constantly fight. Thus, the "Cool It Squad" was born.

I was one of the inaugural members of the "Cool It Squad." We were made up by as wide an array of students as the administration could muster. I am certain that there was a symbolic component to seeing a diverse group roaming the hall together. As far as we were concerned, however, the crew's sole purpose was to maintain order. Today, we would have each been called a "conflict manager" and would have been given multiple trainings, spread over several weeks of role-playing and discussion. As it was, our only rite of passage was a 20-minute presentation, during which I spent the entire time talking. After that, we were sent wherever the administrators thought there might be conflict. This directive meant we were at games, dances, and, most importantly, lunch.

I remember standing in the cafeteria one day and being hailed by a white classmate. "Cool It Squad" members worked in tandems, and so, my buddy—a black guy who was also on the football team—and I wandered over to see what was the problem. The white guy informed me, with language that would shame a sailor, that "the n***** over there" had been saying things to him that were mildly offensive. I looked in the direction my classmate was indicating and saw a black kid, who was eating his lunch alone with his head down. I recalled letting my gaze pause on him as I scanned the lunchroom for conflicts and wondering if I shouldn't sit down and talk to this potentially lonely person.

"You know, I've just seen him eating lunch," I told the accuser.

"Are you kidding?" The guy seemed ready to start into another profanity-laden tirade.

"What'd you see?" I turned to my partner.

My buddy shrugged. "Him eating lunch."

The seated white kid looked at the black guy standing next to me and was poised to drop another 'N-bomb.'

I put my wrist on the table. "I think you're lying."

The accuser looked at me, incredulous.

"Now, why don't you do like that guy's doing and just finish your lunch."

With that, my teammate and I walked away.

The thing was, it was never athletes that the "Cool It Squad" had to worry about. I don't know if it was because we felt as if we were part of the same football family or if it was simply because we didn't want to get suspended and miss a game, but athletes didn't start fights. That doesn't mean, however, that we didn't sometimes find ourselves in the middle of them.

My sophomore year, we were sitting on the bus outside Sequoia High School waiting for the bus driver to put it in gear. Because we were there for a football game, I was focused and pretty well oblivious to everything that was going on around me. So, when a large Hispanic man in a black leather biker jacket came up the stairs and started eyeing the players, I thought nothing of it. Next to me, I heard something "click."

I looked, and my buddy Chris Lueder had his helmet on and was buckling his chinstrap.

"Chris, what are you doing?"

"Mark," Chris said as he finished snapping into his helmet, "we don't have any Mexicans on our team."

I guess I figured that the guy at the front of the bus was an envoy sent by Sequoia High School to ensure they had enough orange slices cut up for us to share on the sidelines. I realized this assumption wasn't the case, about the same time that I noticed I was sitting 10 feet from the guy. Then, outside the bus, all hell broke loose.

Fists began pounding the steel walls that had us enveloped, and coins started pelting the windows. Someone on the back of the bus bigger, tougher, and less oblivious than me must have done something because the Hispanic biker disappeared. The driver hastily shut the door, and we rode out the storm on his newly dented bus.

When it came time for us to play Ravenswood, the school from which we'd collected the majority of our melanin, someone decided that the tension was too high. Because of the forced busing and the revisioning of Ravenswood as a magnet school, both squads were populated with transplants, and players from both sides were going to be playing against people from their own neighborhoods. Administrators decided that this situation was more than the two communities could handle. Subsequently, the game was moved from its traditional Friday night time slot into an afternoon tilt, and no fans were let in. Both sides were allowed six cheerleaders, who, rather than invigorating the crowd, were left to provide spontaneous cries of "Let's go Bob!" and "Keep handing it to'em Mark!"

It was downright eerie.

The most eerie thing during those four years of tumult, however, had nothing to do with violence or even the threat of it. It was at a Thursday night team dessert.

Our high school coach had been doing Thursday night desserts for as long as he had been the head coach. I'm sure that he liked to think of them as bonding experiences for the players, as well as a way for us to coordinate things among ourselves. I say this, because he didn't bring all the parents together before the season and create a schedule of who was going to host each one. Instead, he would simply ask for volunteers on Wednesday the week before and give it to the first player who spoke up. It was then our job to make sure that everybody got there. This undertaking became more complicated when there were players who didn't just live around the corner from each other, but the coach approached it the exact same way.

I never worried about how people were going to get to the desserts—my buddies and I always took care of each other, and we knew the roads of Belmont inside and out. But one Wednesday after practice, the coach posed the same question that he always had but received a different answer.

"So, we've dessert lined up for tomorrow night, but who's going to take it next Thursday?"

"Hey coach," one of the black guys called from among the group, "how come we always have the desserts in Belmont?"

I looked around at my teammates, not wanting to be the one to give what I thought was the obvious answer: because the school's in Belmont. I could tell that they were thinking the same thing I was.

The coach answered the question with a question. "Where do you want to have it?"

"Why can't we have it in East Palo Alto?"

All of the players, including me, looked from the questioner to the coach.

The coach scratched his chin. "We'd need somebody to host it."

We all turned and looked at each other.

"I'll host it, Coach."

"Perfect. Next Thursday night, East Palo Alto."

None of us knew whose house we were going to at that point. We just knew we were going to our pre-game dessert in a town other than our own.

Our team was made up of 45 guys, 12 of whom were black. This situation meant that 33 of us had to pile into cars and drive down highway 101 into East Palo Alto, a town for us that was more than on the other side of the tracks. If Dorothy had been with us, she would have declared that we weren't in Kansas anymore when we looked up and saw a black guy drinking a Coke on a roadside billboard.

Coincidentally (or maybe my teammates from East Palo Alto had planned it that way), the next day's contest was going to be away. In other words, we were wearing our white jerseys. So, when we pulled up to the curb outside the designated dessert domicile, the neighbors were treated to a parade of the whitest boys in the whitest uniforms with the reddest faces that they would ever see. We tried not to pay attention to the blinds that were being held open by fingers as we walked quickly up our teammate's driveway and pounded tentatively on door, hoping it would open quickly.

When we stepped inside the house, it really didn't look any different than any of the homes in Belmont, in which we had been for previous desserts. There were younger siblings who were sitting on the living room furniture, eager to be a part of their brother's high school football team, aunts and uncles in pictures hanging on the walls, and parents putting out trays of cupcakes, cookies, and brownies. Except all of those people were black, and everyone in the house felt awkward. There weren't the jovial conversations, practical jokes, or the relaxed atmosphere that always existed at the other team gatherings.

For the first time, it felt like we were a part of a social experiment.

And, then the parents told us to grab some dessert.

No one ran to the table, but we were all eager to do something. By the time everyone had some sort of sweet in their hands, it felt like any other dessert. We laughed, we prodded, we were reprimanded by assistant coaches, and we received closing remarks from our head coach. Then, we all went home.

I would love to be able to say that on that car trip home that we discussed how what we'd just gone through—entering a different neighborhood, filled with people who looked different than we did—must be what each of our teammates felt every time they hopped on the school bus, but we didn't. I don't know if we weren't smart enough or just not reflective enough to think about it, but we'd just gotten a taste of what they must have felt when the courts decided to integrate the schools. Looking back on it, in some respects, our community made the South look enlightened. There, everyone knew where everybody should and shouldn't go and wasn't afraid to talk about it. On our stretch of Highway 101, nobody said a word about what towns were black and what towns were white. Maybe, that's because we thought there was no segregation on our coast. Or maybe, that was because the highway served as our boundary—white people lived west of 101, black people lived east. We didn't need to talk about it.

But, when our school was integrated, everything changed. Furthermore, it wasn't just for the athletes and students. School buses only ran in the morning. Right after school, athletes with practice had to find their own way home. Nobody that I know of ever talked about how the black kids on our team would get home, but they did. I would imagine that some of the kid's parents drove in and picked them up. I've also gotten the distinct impression that the parents of the white kids drove my teammates back to East Palo Alto. All of a sudden, at least for people associated with the football team, it wasn't black versus white or Belmont versus East Palo Alto anymore—we were all in this together.

Based on the number of fights and the amount of strife felt by the students at our school, I'm certain that some individuals would say that integration was an asinine idea. For those of us who were athletes, however, it changed our perspective on the world. To this day, when I go to Carlmont reunions, about the only black classmates who show up are the athletes. When I take Willamette's football team down to Menlo College for a game, I inevitably run into teammates from the Carlmont squad who have stayed in the Bay Area and think it would be fun to see my team play. We had become bonded together in a way that only people who have faced great adversity could.

So, was it an asinine idea?

Yes.

Was it necessary for the country?

Yes.

And because of it, we all became better men.

Chapter 8 The Long Road to College

While football may have kept me above the social and political fray in high school, it was also what drove me academically. I was by no means a bad student—it wasn't like I was just trying to stay eligible—but whenever I had an assignment that was particularly daunting, I thought about what would happen to me as a football player if I didn't complete it.

I now realize that this mindset was probably cultivated by my family, particularly my father. Football was revered in my household, something that was watched after church every Sunday. In my young mind, it was a part of the sanctity of the Sabbath. Although we didn't have a ton of money, my dad somehow managed to score free tickets to football games. I'm sure that the first few sets of tickets came by way of his father's status in the toy company, but when my dad made friends with several of the (then) Los Angeles Rams players, our experiences with the sport changed dramatically. We would get invited up to hang out in player's hotel rooms, which for an eight-year-old was like passing through a secret portal into a land of giants. The players were like friendly monsters, and it seemed to me that Roman Gabriel—the Ram's Pro Bowl quarterback—had an entire forest growing on his chest. Sometimes, these mythical creatures would leave their world of hotels and stadiums and enter ours.

The Rams defensive line at the time was known as the "Fearsome Foursome," a quartet of behemoths who loved nothing more than sacking the quarterback. (The term "sack" was actually adopted by the league from the description Deacon Jones, the most famous of the group, gave for tackling a quarterback behind the line.) After a game, one of the "Fearsome Foursome" asked if we could beat the bus to the airport. My dad ensured him that we could.

A moment later, three of the Rams defensive linemen were in our station wagon, with Mike and I wedged into the cargo area in the back. The players, confident in my dad's ability to outpace the team bus, had him make a stop at a mini-market. I don't know if it was an attempt to staunch the onset of the aches that would come later that night or the sense that no road trip was complete without alcohol, but when we pulled out of that parking lot, the already stuffed station wagon was more than a couple ounces heavier. On the 20-minute ride to the airport, Mike and I made a game of trying to catch the beer cans as they sailed over the beastly shoulders of the men seated in front of us.

Though it was my dad's connections that helped us experience what the NFL was like behind the scenes, it never really brought us any material rewards. That's what I was good at. When we'd go to baseball games, I would stand at the rail during batting practice and get every autograph I wanted. (Mike would tell you that he started giving me the things that he wanted signed so that he didn't have to stand there and come away empty-handed.) Sometimes after football games, we'd stick around to see the visiting team walk from the locker room to their bus. After a contest against the Oakland Raiders, my dad, brother, and I waited for the San Diego Chargers to make their way out of the stadium, in the hope of getting an autograph or two. We had some success, capturing a few scrawls across our programs, but it wasn't anything special, when compared to our other after-game sessions.

That was until one of the last guys out of the locker room stopped to talk to me.

That guy was Sid Gilman, San Diego's head football coach.

"Hey, you want to get some autographs?"

"Yeah!"

Without a glance to my dad to make sure it was alright, Mike and I trailed Coach Gilman as if he were the proverbial pied piper, leading a band of children on some mischievous trip. We stopped by the cargo bay under the bus where he grabbed a grass stained "Duke" from the bag marked "Game Balls." He handed me the ball and said, "Why don't you get the autographs on this."

We then followed the coach to the double-wide double-doors. The steps, which should have seemed large and steep to a boy of 10, seemed to propel me upwards toward the promised land.

When we were in the cabin, I was bombarded by the sight of shredded tape and ripped muscle, the sound of exhausted sighs and exasperated swears, and the smell of cotton, leather, and flesh, soaked in perspiration. I held the battered ball at my midsection, and Mike and I were ushered down the aisle, pausing at each row for the player to place his autograph on the pigskin. When we got off that bus, we had a game ball with the autograph of every single San Diego Charger and a memory that would last a lifetime.

It's a good thing I still have that memory, because when we got home that day, Mike and I decided we just had to go play catch…with the game ball.

So, there we were, standing in the street out front of my house, scuffing another name off the ball with each dropped pass, and we never gave it a second thought. I realize now that the moments that I had with those players were something on which I could never put a price (and I've done everything I can to avoid determining what that ball would be worth today). Those memories are probably why I fell in love with football, and part of the reason why I have made it my career. Football, for me, has produced a lifetime of great moments.

✦ ✦ ✦

The other thing about football, more than any other sport, is the importance of hustle. In basketball and baseball, more often than not, nuance is a part of what you do—you're having to feather in a lay-up or patiently take a pitch to the opposite field. I realize that these sort of adjustments help define the modern quarterback, but then playing that position was never really in the cards for me. For everybody else on the field, if you can hustle, you can play.

I remember realizing this fact during the games we'd play in the streets around Belmont. The field was the street in front of my house (it was chosen because it was the flattest area in a hilly neighborhood), the curb was out of bounds, and the lamp posts marked the end zones. The cars, which we could never count on to be parked in the same place or in the same numbers as the night before, were simply a part of the field, land mines that most players chose to avoid. For me, it was as if they didn't exist. Any ball that was in the air, it was mine. It didn't matter if I had to slam into bumpers or dive over hoods; I was going to come away with the catch.

We began to use my reckless abandon as a strategy, lining me up across from someone who was less committed (in this context, the word may take on additional meanings) and throwing the ball to spots where we knew the defender wouldn't be willing to go. I am sure that the older kids took advantage of me on occasion, just to see how far I would go for the catch, but Mike was always there to reel them back in. He took to calling routes that had me leaping into bushes instead of Buicks, which served the dual purpose of protecting his little brother and sending him into fits of laughter when I would come up with mouthfuls of juniper berries.

By the time I was able to play Pop Warner, I was certain I would be able to do anything the coaches asked of me. They just weren't going to be able to ask the kid with no hands to carry the ball. At any other point in my life, I would have taken offense—who were they to say what I could or couldn't do?—but for once, I didn't set out to prove them wrong. This situation wasn't because I was scared that I would fail—I was one of the stars of our neighborhood football league—or because I thought that I was too small to take the punishment (though I was one of the smallest kids on the team). Instead, it was because I was too excited to do the one thing we couldn't do in the streets outside my house: tackle people.

After I explained to my coaches that I didn't want to play with my hooks, they decided that a kid with no hands would make a perfect lineman—I'd never get handed a holding penalty. What they didn't expect was how quick I would be getting to the ball. I can't tell you if it was that I was faster than the other players, if years of playing with my older brother had given me an eye for the game that the others lacked, or if as a defensive tackle, I was simply closer to the play's origin than any of the other players, but coaches always seemed impressed with how I was the first one to the ballcarrier. That attribute would bode well for me in high school.

By the time I was a freshman, I was certain, with three years of experience, that I was going to have a leg-up on my competition for a spot on the defensive line. The problem was, the other players vying for the spot had a full head (and 30 pounds) on me. The coaches, much to my chagrin, moved me to linebacker, which I realized was still populated by players taller and heavier than me. I was uncomfortable. I was small, I was yards away from the ball, and there was no one for me to immediately hit. And, I loved it.

All of a sudden, instead of my attempts at tackling being desperate swipes at a running back's ankles, I was free to move, to track the play, and to explode into ballcarriers. By the second game of my freshman year, I was feeling pretty good about myself and my new position. Furthermore, it was in that game that I received the greatest compliment that I ever received as a player.

Our opponent had virtually no passing attack. In other words, I had to only worry about their running game. It was a linebacker's dream. It was also an umpire's dream. (Positioned directly behind the inside linebackers, the umpire's job is to watch the offensive and defensive lines for holding penalties. This chore is much more difficult when teams are always throwing the ball, sometimes at your head.) As a new linebacker, I hardly knew that the umpire existed. The only reason I even noticed that game's umpire was because he was bigger than any referee I'd seen. Still, I went about my business and managed to have the game of my life, registering 26 tackles (most of which were five yards down field, but who's counting?). After the gun sounded and before I could line up to shake hands with the other team, the oversized umpire pulled me aside and told me I'd played the best game he'd ever seen out of a linebacker and that he ought to know. Just as he was about to tell me his name, I recognized him.

"Leo Nommelini!"

Standing before me was the Hall of Fame former offensive lineman and linebacker for the San Francisco 49ers, complimenting me on my play. I was lucky that I didn't die on the spot.

As you might imagine, this did wonders for my confidence. Unfortunately, I was already confident—the only place for me to go was to move into the realm of cocky. Over the years, I have learned that having this outlook is not a good place to be. Unfortunately, it would take a heavy dose of humility, before I would learn the lesson for good.

That very next week, our coach decided that we needed some toughening up. At the high school level, this has always meant pitting the sophomores against the freshmen the day before the next game. This story line was a big deal for us, and as the cocksure leader of the defense, I made sure everyone felt ready. Unfortunately, you can only prepare for so many scenarios. My shoulder proved unready for an odd landing that I had after a tackle. The pain exploded in my arm. It was like nothing that I'd ever felt before or since. It was excruciating. Fortunately, like an athlete's best friend, numbness ushered the pain away, and I continued in the scrimmage.

By the time we got to the locker room, I knew I'd need help getting out of my shoulder pads. Though it didn't hurt, I knew something was still wrong. My shoulder was stiff, and when I moved it, it sounded like a truck, filled with broken glass driving down a gravel road. The coach, after having a listen, determined that I'd be able to play the next day, but only with some additional equipment. He then disappeared into the equipment closet and came out with a couple different sizes of half-inch thick foam donuts.

It was like he'd brought a box of band-aids to a 14-car pile-up.

When my dad came by to get me, all he needed to hear was a single crunch. We were off to the hospital for x-rays.

I remember sitting in that consultation room, my anxiety reflecting off the stark white walls and back onto me. Was I ever going to be able to play football again? Was I even going to be able to move my arm the same way again?

Finally, the door opened.

"Oh, I want to be a football hero," the doctor sang as he threw the x-rays up on the backlit screen.

The first pictures that he showed us were of my good shoulder. He pointed out my collar bone, humerus, and the ball and socket that made up the shoulder joint. Then he put up the pictures of my injured shoulder. Something seemed to be missing. There was no ball in the socket. The doctor explained that my shoulder had dislocated, separated, and been broken. The ball that I had been unable to find was in my armpit.

At that point, I knew that the pad my coach had given me wasn't going to help. I was devastated. I wasn't going to be playing in the next day's game. That was the least of my parents' worries.

By the time I got home, both my mom and dad were throwing fits.

"Is he going to have full range of motion?"

"Will he be able to open a door or eat his lunch?"

"Is he going to be able to use his hooks?"

"Is he going to be able to live a normal life?"

"I don't know about all that, but his football career is certainly over."

Thankfully, my mom calmed down. As she had all my life, she decided that I would figure out a way to make it work. I would get someone to help me around school, someone to help me eat lunch, and someone to help me in class. That was just how it was going to be.

And, that was just how it was.

People would just volunteer to get the door and take my notes. It wasn't just my teammates—I had girls feed me at lunch. Not just stuffing sandwiches in my mouth, but daintily wiping my face after each bite. For a guy who was self-conscious talking to people of the opposite sex, breaking my arm was the most effective flirting technique that I had ever deployed. But, alas, I got better.

After two surgeries—one to put in pins, one to take them out—I began to notice my range of motion returning. It seemed that I was able to do everything again, but the question remained: would I be able to play football again?

I don't know if that doctor was an old-school curmudgeon or a forward-thinking dynamo, but he gave me that plainest answer in the annals of sports medicine—if it doesn't hurt, you can play. I decided I was going to play.

The thing that I didn't realize until my sophomore season was about to start was how much I *didn't* want to have contact. Yeah, I'd spent all winter, spring, and summer working out with the team (doing my own program), and I loved my teammates. The thought of actually playing, however, scared me. I wasn't sure that my shoulder was fully recovered, and I was certain I did not want to go through surgery again (unless I received a guarantee that the girls would feed me).

Still, by that first padded practice, all of the varsity coaches had heard of my exploits on the freshman team, and they were having me mix it up with them. Oddly enough, they had me in at running back, and the play had me running a passing route. I swung out to the right, running as fast as I could because I was a sophomore on the varsity who wanted to show that I belonged. I was certain, however, that the ball was never going to be thrown my way. Yet, as I turned my route upfield, I saw the ball had been lofted in my direction. It was a bit behind me, and all I could manage to get on it was my left arm. Somehow, in the manner of David Tyree's miracle catch in the Super Bowl in which the Giants beat the Patriots, I managed to pin the ball against my helmet. There was no time to be proud of myself. For the moment, however, I had trapped the ball. At that point, my buddy Chris Lueder—one of the only other sophomores on the varsity team—unloaded on me. It was a hellacious hit that lifted me clean in the air. When Chris landed on top of me, I didn't think that there was a molecule of oxygen left in my lungs. Yet, somehow I'd managed to hang on to the ball.

The entire team rushed from the field and sideline, hooting and hollering the whole way.

"What a hit!"

"Attaboy, Chris!"

"He'll feel that one tomorrow!"

And, not a word, from a coach or a player, about the one-handed catch made by the guy with no hands. I realized then that I'd made it.

Strangely enough, it was that play that brought an end to the coaches' experimentation with me as a ballcarrier. To that point in my career, I'd always played running back, as el as wide receiver on occasion. (At my freshman coach's retirement dinner, I spoke and said that, while I appreciated everything that he'd done for me, I too had gone on and become a coach and had come to the conclusion that I liked my receivers to have hands.)

They weren't giving up on me as a linebacker, but they'd found a new position for me—offensive line. This decision might seem counter-intuitive for a guy who was still a bit averse to contact, but playing offensive line was a God-send. I wasn't going to be building up huge heads of steam in order to pile drive ballcarriers with my shoulder. Instead, I was going to get a step or two before I made contact, and then, it was going to be with my forearms. The onus of constantly wondering if my shoulder would be okay was gone; I was going to be able to enjoy football, as well as my teammates.

My shoulder issues out of my mind, and my position as pulling guard secured, I began to get a bit of my swagger back. I think my brother knew it, because he and his water-polo teammates started to give me a harder and harder time as I would walk past their pool on the way in from practice. One day, having suffered one too many indignations from a barrage of splashing water-polo players, I told my brother's entire team what I'd been telling him for weeks at home—I could step in that pool and be the best shallow end goalie they had. Mike looked around the pool and, getting nods from everyone (including his coach), he invited me in.

After stripping down to my girdle, I climbed in the pool to the catcalls of both my teammates and Mike's. I subsequently made my way to the goal that was positioned where the water was four feet deep. By the time I had turned around, a shooting line had formed; it felt like they were each waiting their turn at the county fair to dunk the guy who was already in the water. They couldn't have been more than 10 yards away, but that seemed like a reasonable distance from which a water polo player would take a shot. I nodded to let them know I was ready. Mike was the first guy in line. He hurled the ball right at me. I swatted it away and smiled. The next guy tried to put one over my shoulder. I rejected it with ease. I bounced on my toes, wondering with how much flair I could stop the next one. The third guy threw the ball directly into the water. I remember thinking, *well, that was stu*—and then getting drilled in the nose. It was as if the ball had accelerated as it skipped off the water and upon impact with my face, it caused me to forget where I was for a second. I was still in shock as I watched glops of viscous red liquid begin to hit the water. The pain in my nose brought me back to reality, and I began to hear the laughter from Mike and his teammates.

"That's enough boys," the water polo coach said, looking from me to Mike and back to me. "And make sure you get that checked out."

That bloodied nose was the most trauma my body suffered my entire sophomore season. It felt like it was a success. My shoulder didn't hurt, and I'd practiced with the varsity and started on the JV team. As such, I should have been completely looking forward to my junior year. Something in my mind, however, must have been telling me that neither my coaches nor I had really challenged my shoulder; I hadn't played linebacker yet. I was okay with that. I kind of figured that I'd go through my last two years as a pulling guard, maybe be a captain my senior year, and be able to look back and someday tell my son that I'd managed to overcome the adversity of injury. That story would have been true—outwardly. On the other hand, if I had never played linebacker again, I would have always wondered to myself, "what if?" It ended up being a question that I didn't have to ask, but the answer came at the time when I least expected it.

My junior year started off just as I had planned it—I was a leader on the offensive line, and I was playing absolutely no defense. By the third game of the season, our team's depth at linebacker was starting to get a bit thin, but I wasn't getting any work on it at practice. We were set to play against a team chock full of scary seniors, with the ringleader being their tailback who had verbally committed to playing at Oklahoma. This kid was big and fast, and my buddies and I were certain we were going to see something special out of him on that Friday night. When they got the ball for their first possession, I had taken up a prime position on the sideline so I could see how good he really was. The first play took him directly into the line, and he disappeared into the pile. The whistle blew and I watched as everyone rolled off and walked back to their respective huddles, everyone except our starting middle linebacker.

"Speckman!"

Why was the coach hollering my name? I looked down to check and see if I was standing on the headphone cord.

"Speckman, get in there at linebacker!"

Get in there at linebacker? I nearly dropped my helmet, but somehow I managed to put it on as I sprinted out onto the field.

When I got in the huddle, someone was mumbling something about what we were going to do defensively, but I had no clue. I hadn't been on that side of the ball in weeks.

I watched our coaches help our injured linebacker to the sidelines, and I found myself wondering if he had hurt himself hitting the other team's tailback. I peered into their huddle to see if the back was any worse for wear. Instead, he appeared to be bouncing on the balls of his feet.

A moment later, the whistle blew. We broke the huddle, and I waited to see in what formation they would come out. Not surprisingly, it was an I formation, and I figured they'd probably run a toss to the wideside of the formation. I figured that if I was lucky, I'd get blocked before I had to try to make a tackle, our other linebacker would come jogging back in after the play, and I would be able to take my place back on the sideline, waiting for that tailback to do something spectacular.

When the ball was snapped, I immediately read pass. I took a drop, and, with no one in my zone, I took a peek to see where the quarterback was looking. He was turned toward our bench, and he lofted a pass toward the sideline. I started sprinting in that direction before I realized that the tailback was the target. He brought the ball down in the flat and began his move upfield. I remembered a coach once telling me that if I was going to make a mistake that I should make it full speed. A plan formed in my mind—I was going to run right where that tailback would be if he stayed on the same path, launch myself into what I hoped would look like a diving tackle from two yards away, miss gloriously, slide into our coaches' box, and get pulled on the spot. It was perfect.

The strange thing was that tailback stayed on the same path. I don't know if my teammates were pursuing him so he couldn't cut back or if he simply thought he could run me over, but he surely wasn't ready for the 155-pound sideline missile my body had become. Subsequently, before either one of us knew what was happening, my surgically repaired shoulder caught him just below the knee, flipping him over and ending the play on the spot.

My plan for skidding into our coaches' box had nearly worked, for when I came to a stop, it was my coach picking me up off the turf and putting his face inches from my facemask.

"Speckman, I knew you could do it! You're the best hitter we got!"

He pounded me on my bad shoulder, and I ran back out to the huddle.

I never thought about that shoulder again.

By the end of my senior season, I was beginning to realize that I was at the end of my football career. In four years of high school football, I'd managed to learn how to play two new positions, to recover from two significant injuries (I tore the cartilage in my knee in the spring of my junior year), and to find a sport where I could compete against anyone. Now, it was about to be over.

I remember sitting in the locker room after that final game with tears in my eyes, struggling to keep my labored breaths from turning into sobs. My coach came over to me, put his hand on my sweaty back, and asked what was wrong. I lost it.

"Th-th-this is it coach. I-I-I'm never going to play football again."

He sat down next to me and looked into my bleary eyes. "What do you mean?"

I took a deep breath. "I'm a s-s-senior. I'm graduating this spring."

"I know that Speckman, but you're going to play next year. I can think of plenty of schools that can use you."

I wiped my eyes and looked at him with new clarity. "Really?"

"Oh yeah. Come by my office Monday. We'll see what we can find for you."

My career had been granted clemency. Even though we still needed to find a school that wanted a linebacker with no hands, it was my high school coach who had saved my career. My shoulder wasn't right until he showed me it was, and I wasn't good enough to keep playing football until he told me I was. So, while it was Menlo and Azusa Pacific Colleges that extended my playing career another four years, it was my high school coach who turned football into my life's passion. Football showed that I could compete with anybody. It was my coach, however, who made me believe I could. It's a legacy I hope to perpetuate.

Chapter 9 I Made It! (Now What Do I Do?)

Once my coach had convinced me that I could play in college, I had to figure out where I would go. I was pretty sure that if I was going to go to a junior college, I wanted to live at home (to save money). As a result, I was able to quickly narrow down my choices. Seven miles in one direction was the College of San Mateo where my brother Mike attended and played water polo. It was an inexpensive public school. Ten miles in the other direction was Menlo College, an expensive private school known as the back door to Stanford. Both sounded appealing, so I did as I counsel recruits to this day: I went to the schools to see them both firsthand.

The luster quickly wore off College of San Mateo after I'd gone to the campus to visit Mike and worked out with the football team. It had nothing to do with the coaches. They were first rate. It had nothing to do with the players; they accepted me as one of their own. It also had nothing to do with the program—they seemed to win the league every year. It had to do with what all of that meant: 120 players on the squad, with a depth chart at my position that would have intimidated someone 20 pounds heavier, two inches taller, and two tenths of a second faster than me. At College of San Mateo, my dreams of playing college football would have played out on a practice field. I decided I'd best check out Menlo.

Menlo was the only private junior college in California, and with a small campus and smaller student body, I wasn't surprised that their football team wasn't especially large—40 guys. If I went there, I would have a chance to compete for a starting job, and might be able to get myself on film that I could send off to Stanford. I was sold. Thankfully, Menlo was sold on me. I didn't realize that private equals expensive, when I made my decision. Accordingly, when I received a letter during the third week of school letting me know that a scholarship was going to pay my tuition, I was a bit surprised, as well as grateful.

The summer before school started, I arrived at Menlo for the start of camp, as nervous as I've ever been. I wasn't sleeping much, and when I was, it was fitful. I wished I could have said that I was feeling the same things as every other freshman. Was I going to make some friends? Was I going to like my roommate? Was I going to be able to compete at this level? In reality, I wasn't.

I was worried because I had no idea who was going to tie all of the laces on all of my pieces of equipment. In high school, my friends had always been happy to do it, but they'd known me for years. This situation was the first time that my new teammates were going to see me, a guy with no hands, competing with them for a job.

So, my initial thought was that I would have the coaches help me since they were the ones who, at least, knew who I was, but I discovered too late that they were nowhere to be seen in the few minutes before practice. My second thought was that I would discover a method that would work now that I was about to embark on my journey into higher education. I was in college. I was going to be able to figure out things that were twice as difficult and at twice the rate. (Needless to say, I still can't tie my shoes.) My third thought was that Walt Disney would appear with a cast of animated singing mice and would sprinkle pixie dust on every one of my laces allowing them to tie themselves. Walt, however, didn't oblige my fantasy. As a result, I was forced to turn to the stranger next to me who'd already managed to get all of his gear on.

"Hey, do you think you can tie my girdle?"

The guy looked from my face to my girdle and back up to my face. "Are you kidding?"

I shook my head and shrugged.

With a sigh that said, *this guy can't even tie his own shit*, my teammate reluctantly tied my girdle.

"Thank you." I swallowed hard. "How about my shoes?"

Despite both of our embarrassment, I somehow managed to get him to tie everything for me on that first day of practice. At that point, I decided right then and there that I was going to win a starting job, if for no other reason than to show how capable I was on the field, even if I seemed incapable off of it.

I won the starting job.

◆ ◆ ◆

It was before my first game at Menlo that I realized I had really *earned* my spot on the defense. All during camp, I'd watched as Ray Solari, our head coach, had pushed everyone to the limit—physically and mentally. We'd go for three hours without water breaks. He'd step into drills to illustrate how to be violent. Furthermore, he'd told me on more than one occasion that he "liked to slow guys down during practice, not speed them up." It was the hardest I'd ever been pushed, and I can't say that I enjoyed it.

Subsequently, I decided that as long as I had gear on, I was going to go as fast as I could, and that I was going to make it, so that Coach Solari would never have to show me how to do anything remotely physical. Still, after three weeks of grueling practices, Solari's perspective on the game didn't fully crystallize for me until he gathered us together in the locker room, minutes before kickoff.

"Booth, get up here."

Booth, our captain, stood up from among the kneeling players and approached Coach Solari.

The two faced each other. There was a glimmer in both of their eyes and a febrile intensity to their set jaws. It reminded me of two heavyweights, waiting for the referee to finish his pre-fight instructions.

"Give me a shot sir!"

Coach Solari wound up and slapped Booth across the face.

My jaw dropped. What the hell was going on? I looked around at the crowd. Some of my fellow freshmen were doing the same. The sophomores reacted with an expectant murmur.

"Give me a shot!"

I watched as Booth hauled off and slapped Coach Solari.

"Yeah!"

"Yeah!"

"Let's go!"

I felt myself swept up in the moment and charged into the bouncing mass, allowing my body to be carried out in a sea of emotional momentum, even as my mind swam in a sea of uncertainty. I still remember the one thought that was going through my mind as I prepared to take my first collegiate snap: *What the hell just happened?*

Though that first game was a blur, it had become apparent that Coach Solari was passionate not only about football, but about our team. In other words, no matter who you were, you could either move up the depth chart or down the depth chart, based solely on your performance. It was the ultimate meritocracy, and Coach Solari lorded over it as such. Luckily, my performance each week was good enough to keep me in the lineup.

Subsequently, when the newspapers started to send reporters to Menlo, curious about the linebacker with no hands, Coach Solari was having no part of it. He could often be heard repeating the refrain, "I play Mark because he is one of the two best linebackers on the team." For him, it never mattered; in fact I began to wonder if the reporters hadn't shown up if he would even have noticed that I didn't have hands.

By the end of my freshman season, I realized that I was beginning to come into my own. I'd started every game and watched myself improve as a linebacker. In addition, the Nautilus® and the Universal Gym systems in the weight room allowed me to not only lift with the team, but be on the same program. Furthermore, I was getting the best grades of my life.

You would think that I would have been happy. I wasn't. Something just didn't feel right. My gut told me it was Menlo, and I kept checking in at College of San Mateo, certain that they'd seen me on film and would jump at the chance to add one of Menlo's starting linebackers to their squad. Instead, their roster was only getting bigger (in every possible way), and though I had added some bulk, to them I was still a small guy with no hands, who wasn't worth a scholarship. That scenario put transferring out of the question.

Thank God.

If I had been able to transfer, I may have been happier initially, but I would have never gotten to the root of my melancholy. I came to realize (over the course of several half-hour drives between school and home) that Menlo had nothing to do with my frustration. I was finally tired of using my absence of hands as a motivator. Yes, the desire to prove everyone wrong had served me well, but suddenly, I wanted to know what was the cost? I had felt myself growing more and more bitter with each passing year, and from that bitterness were coming bursts of anger and sarcasm.

I hadn't alienated anyone, but I had been so intent on showing everyone what a great student and player the guy with no hands could be that I hadn't shown anybody what a great *person* I could be. I realized that I didn't want to answer the questions about my lack of digits with witty retorts any more—that only served to sensationalize a relatively small physical characteristic that made up a fraction of who I am. I was going to take all questions and answer them the same way Coach Solari had—in a straightforward manner, and if anyone was intent on bringing attention to me, I was going to make sure that it was because I deserved it.

The emotional weight that had been lifted freed me in a way that no tool or trick ever had. I began to seek out things to try, just because they seemed interesting, not because they seemed like an opportunity to show the world. That spring, the talk around Coach Solari's office was of how many tournaments Jimmy Connors would win.

At the time, the must-have piece of sporting equipment was, of course, the Jimmy Connors model tennis racquet. It had a large open "V," stretching from the head of the racquet to the handle. I wondered if I wouldn't be able to jury-rig a way to make it work for me. I'd always appreciated tennis, but never thought it was a sport that I could play. With my new mindset, however, I figured if I cradled the handle in my left armpit and put my right wrist through the notch, I would be able to swing it without it flying all over the court each time I hit a shot. (My technique became refined when I decided to use inside-out athletic tape to add some additional adhesion.)

The results were much better than I thought possible. Eventually, I began playing frequently with other guys from the team. One day, Coach Solari walked by as I was playing and stopped to watch a point. I managed a couple of good ground strokes before putting it into the net. I looked up to see my coach's take on the matter.

"Hey, that's pretty good Specky. Let me know when you can play the piano."

That line still brings a smile to my face. It was then that I knew I had not only rediscovered myself, but I was ready to grow as a person.

My resolve was tested immediately my sophomore year. I'd decided to live on campus. As a former homebody, I was amazed at how loudly people could listen to music and how much people could drink. This scenario wasn't just at house parties. It also wasn't just on Friday nights. I never knew if, when I dropped off my books on the way to practice, I would have to decline an afternoon invitation for a "session" with somebody in the dorm.

The locker room seemed like a perfect sanctuary as I made this transition. I'd been named captain. Furthermore, because of my new weight-training program, I was stronger and faster than I'd ever been. The only concern I had was whether Coach Solari and I were going to have to trade shots, but without saying a word to each other, we concluded that was one tradition that would be put on hold for a year. With that worry out of the way, life on the field was wonderful—for the first two weeks.

By the third week of the season, I had come to terms with the sophomoric partying of my classmates and had managed to work out a schedule for studying around them. It seemed like fate was ready for me to become the man I'd promised myself I'd become.

Then, during that third game of the year, I separated the cartilage in my sternum.

This injury was nothing like my shoulder—I didn't just think something was wrong, I knew it was. Running hurt, walking hurt, even breathing hurt. On top of that, I tore several ligaments in my foot. That could have very easily have been the end of my playing career, but the ethos of football then (and to a lesser degree now) was that you figured out a way to play hurt. For our school, that meant the horse cream DMSO.

At the time, Menlo was one of two schools in California that was licensed to use this topical painkiller. Furthermore, the trainers used it liberally. Bruise? You got it. Finger dislocation? No problem. Sore throat? Stick out your tongue. This cure-all would have seemed exciting to me had the ointment not stunk to high heaven. If you were using DMSO, everyone within a one-block radius knew it. I had returned to my position as the elephant in the room, only this time as a seemingly flatulent one. Thanks to the cream, however, I could run well enough by Thursday to get through practice, and by Saturday I could play.

I can't say that the season was magical after that, but it was certainly memorable. During one game, I intercepted the pass of Tom Craft, who went on to become the long-time head coach of San Diego State University. After returning the ball up the sidelines,

I stepped out of bounds before I could get tackled in hopes of sparing my sternum the unnecessary contact. Tom, angry that he'd been picked off by an injured guy with no hands, plowed into me over a yard onto the sidelines, drawing an unnecessary roughness penalty. I still give him flack about it to this day. A couple of the papers in the area ran flattering stories about what I was accomplishing on the field. And at our post-season banquet, I was informed that I'd been named 2nd team All-League, as voted by opposing coaches, and had been picked as the Most Courageous by my teammates for playing hurt. They were the first two awards that I'd ever received, based solely on my play; they had nothing to do with whether or not I had hands.

Apparently, not only was I ready to forget about my handicap, so was the rest of world.

Chapter 10 Ball and Band: The Life of a Football-Playing Musician

After my sophomore season, I was pretty sure that I was done with football. I'd not only proven to myself that I could play college football, but that I could play at a high level. At that point, my under-sized body was telling me it was enough. Though my sternum and feet hadn't gotten worse during the season, they hadn't gotten better either. The energy it had taken to fight through the pain seemed to have left me when the whistle had blown on the last play. Coach Solari had made it clear to me that Menlo may have been the back door to Stanford, but for short and small linebackers, it wasn't an all-access pass to the football program. I then realized that I was ready for it to be over. It was time for me to move on.

As I prepared for my last semester at Menlo and my life after football, I would get called in periodically to Coach Solari's office. Sometimes, it was just to chat, and sometimes it was to ask me how my tennis game was coming along, but the topic was never football. One day, however, he asked me about a guy he was recruiting from my *alma mater*, Carlmont High School. I said I knew him well—he was a star running back and had been all over the newspapers.

"He won the Mark Speckman Award."

I blinked hard. "The what?"

Coach Solari smiled. "The Mark Speckman Award. It goes to the most inspirational player on Carlmont's team."

I swallowed hard. *The Mark Speckman Award?* "Really?"

"That's what it says here on his information sheet."

Coach Solari handed me the paper.

"I thought that you had to be dead to have an award named after you."

"So did I." I looked at the information sheet. Sure enough, it said 'recipient of the Mark Speckman Award.' "I knew I won the 'Most Inspirational Player' award my senior year, and they told me they were going to name it after me, but I thought they were joking."

"Well, let me know if you remember anything else about this guy."

I looked up and saw that Coach Solari had a prideful smirk on his face. "I will coach."

♦ ♦ ♦

I can't say that conversation changed my mind about the prospect of playing football again, but it put it back on my radar screen. My body had begun to heal, and there was a buzz around the dorms about where some of my teammates might be heading next. Finally, when I got up the nerve to ask Coach Solari about where I might be able to play, he reiterated it wouldn't be Stanford, and he told me that he hadn't gotten any calls about me. Before I could become disheartened, he reminded me that he also hadn't recruited me. Look what good it had done him. He promised to make some calls and that we'd put together some film of me to shop around.

I left his office excited. Football might not be over for me yet.

Picking a school for my junior and senior years was relatively easy. Even though there were more than 20 small schools with football teams in California, not every one of them was interested in a player who was marketing himself, especially one who was physically incapable of glad-handing. Of those who expressed even a modicum of interest, I really only liked one: Azusa Pacific. It wasn't their coaching staff that wooed me, though they were terrific when I got there, and it wasn't the players, though they couldn't have been more accepting. It wasn't their facilities, which were put to shame by Menlo's. Furthermore, it wasn't their Southern California location—no self-respecting citizen of the bay area would admit to that. It was simply that, even though I had managed to accept the culture of Menlo for what it was, I needed to go somewhere that was more reserved, and Azusa Pacific more than fit the bill.

For starters, Azusa was a highly Christian school. There was a church on campus, with multiple Sunday services, and, as a former altar boy, it reminded me a little bit of home. This setting also meant that there were no co-ed dorms and visiting hours were strictly enforced, curtailing much of the potential for late-night partying. The only way at Azusa that you were even going to get to see a girl past 10 o'clock was if you were married to her, and for this, the school was very accommodating. Ample married housing existed in and around campus. It could be reasonably argued that students were *encouraged* to get married while in school.

With an immediate comfort level established, I was ready to sign on the dotted line. The only problem was, among all the things that I'd learned about the world and myself at Menlo, I still had yet to figure out how I was going to pay to go to this private school. I knew I was going to get some money as a football player and I knew that I was going to be getting a 25-dollar-a-month check from my step grandma, which was what I was going to live on. Beyond that, however, I had no idea. I figured that I could take out loans, but the prospect of that burden when I had no idea what I was going to do when I graduated seemed like more than I could bear. That was when a girl whom I'd played with in a band back at Menlo told me the school needed a trombone player for the traveling band. After discovering that with the position came some scholarship money, I decided to audition. When I was offered the spot, I knew I was headed for Azusa.

Come that August of 1975, I was in the same position as I had been two years before—sitting in a locker room, anxiously awaiting my first practice with a new team. I'd matured a lot in the past two years. While there had been no sleepless nights leading up to this moment, I now was wondering if there should have been. I had on my girdle, my pants, and my pads, and I was looking nervously from player to player. None would make eye contact with me. Perhaps, they weren't looking at me because I was the new guy or maybe they were just mentally preparing themselves for the beginning of what promised to be a grueling camp in the Southern California heat.

Everyone who was near me, however, was silent. In my estimation, they were all doing what I was doing: praying that their equipment held up—not in the sense that it stayed in place (I'd already gotten somebody to tie me up), but held up to contact. The cloth on the shoulder pads was threadbare, and my hip, thigh, and knee pads were little more than sheets of paper, made of compressed foam. In order to assuage my concerns, I'd stopped by the equipment room to see if I could pick up a neck-roll to attach to my shoulder pads. The trainer's response to my request was a rolled up towel held in position by athletic tape. I'd gotten the impression from the coaches on my recruiting trip that they were old school-type coaches—apparently that methodology permeated the program in every capacity.

As someone who appreciated the virtues of both the old and new school's of thought (as well as having a general appreciation for my own well-being), I decided that I could find a solution. Rather than mention my concerns to the coaches I'd known for an afternoon, I contacted some family friends who worked at a local high school to see if I could borrow a pair of their pads. They consented, and, before my next practice with the team, I picked up the equipment and dropped it off in my locker. You have never seen more jealous people than my teammates were when I was strapping up.

"Hey man, where'd you get that stuff?"

"Did you use some scholarship check to go buy some new gear?"

"No," I pulled up my pants, "I borrowed it from the high school."

"The high school? Really?"

I shrugged. "Yeah."

"Well, I'm not tying your pants up unless you give me them thigh pads."

After negotiating my way into keeping all of my borrowed gear, I was off to practice, comfortable that I was going to be able to make it through a day physically.

I had no idea that making it through the day mentally was going to be the bigger challenge during my time at Azusa.

◆ ◆ ◆

I'm pretty sure that the world thinks that being a musician and an athlete are mutually exclusive. Aside from charity basketball games and benefit concerts (which, if you've ever attended either, serves only to bolster that assumption), most people never consider that it is possible to perform in both endeavors. Or at least that's the way it felt for me when looking at the band and football schedules at Azusa.

When school finally got started my junior year, I discovered that we had band practice from 2:30 to 3:30. The football practice time had already been established at 3:15, so as a dual-scholarship musician/athlete, I was in a bit of a pickle. Because necessity, as they say, is the mother of all invention, I immediately went to scheming. I first asked the coach if it would be okay to miss our 15-minute warm-up session that began practice. After receiving his blessing, I was able to negotiate an early (albeit five minute) release from band practice. This schedule bought me five minutes to get from band to football. It was a straight shot, a one-mile drive to the stadium from the music building. Fortunately, on most days, I was able to get a parking spot reasonably close to minimize my jog to the car. Between leaving band and getting to the stadium, I was looking at four minutes. That timetable left me with one minute to get dressed for practice. Plenty of time. Let the madness begin.

Walking into a band practice for the first time is a bit nerve-racking. People are in clusters, and each cluster has its own vibe. Some are busy tuning up, riffing as their instruments become ready. Others are talking about the music that they wish the director had picked and making fun of him for the choices that he ultimately made. Still others are gossiping about everything but music.

Picking your initial clique can be critical to your acceptance by the band members. To state that it is a stressful time would be an understatement. So, when I walked into that first practice wearing my practice pants (stuffed full of pads) and cleats, I had pretty much mailed in any prospect of fitting in with anyone. I was just trying to play some music, find someone to take my instrument home, and get to the stadium on time. I figured that if I ended up being the fodder for the gossipers for only half the pre-practice chatting I was doing well.

Thankfully, I discovered a guy whom I had in a couple other classes who lived close to me who was in the band. My instrument was taken care of. I also realized that band practice was more than wrapping up when I had to leave. As a result, the situation didn't make me feel too conspicuous as I slipped out (although my cleats did). Furthermore, I found out that all of our planned concerts were on Sundays. In other words, there would be no conflicts with football games. It seemed as if I would be home free.

And for the most part, I was.

❖ ❖ ❖

Being a part of both the band and the football team was awesome. Between the two of them, I must have seen nearly every venue for performance in Southern California. On Saturdays, I visited stadiums; on Sundays, churches. My week was organized into morning classes, afternoon practices, and evening study sessions. I had defensive audibles and music to memorize. I also discovered that the claustrophobic confines of a soundproof music practice room served me well for both purposes. I was finding unbelievable opportunities (playing a dawn concert at the Grand Canyon—but don't expect to be able to tune a trombone in sub-freezing temperatures)—and personal success (my senior year, I was an honorable mention All-American football player). Even when a conflict between the two occurred (i.e., a game and concert on the same day), I found a way to make it work (a buddy drove me two hours from the game to the concert; I was the first trombone player on record to expose a bruise on his forearm every time he reached sixth position). It was a terrific life. When it was over, however, I had no idea what I was going to do.

Chapter 11 Life, Liberty, and the Pursuit of Gainful Employment

As someone who has coached football for more than 30 years at this point in my life (you might say that I'm starting to get a bit long in the tooth, but then who would notice that on me?), I can tell you there are times when I have to make a decision, and there are times when decisions are made for me. That I became a coach is a perfect example of a decision being made for me.

During my senior year at Azusa, two things were the talk of the team. The first was me.

On Monday of the week leading up to our first game, I entered the locker room, ready to move onto my in-season routine. Some of the guys were already there, but rather than being spread out among their lockers, they were clustered together, some of them laughing, but all of them poring over something lying on the bench. As I walked over to join them, I watched as a series of nudges silenced the chuckles, and everyone avoided eye contact with me. Before I could ask what was going on, one of the guys said, "You made the newspaper, Speckman." He tossed a flimsy heap of papers my way. The shape of the paper reminded me of a tabloid. The giant headline, "Nostradamus Predicts: End of the World the Week After Next" was almost certainly tabloid. The picture of me on page seven, with the caption "Linebacker Plays With No Hands!" didn't, however, necessarily mean it was a tabloid.

"Hey, can you get me Bat-Boy's autograph?"

"Do you think I can get my picture taken with the man who ate his own face?"

It was a tabloid.

The Star to be exact.

I had gone international.

Whoever said any press is good press was a big fat liar.

The second thing that was the talk of the team was the World Football League (WFL). It had somehow managed to survive its infancy in the shadow of the NFL. Even though it had yet to garner the same popularity or attract the marquee players, it had been steadily growing in stature during its several years of existence. Like most college seniors, the guys on the team were worried about what they would do the next year. For many of them, however, the WFL seemed like the best option. I had no delusions of taking my now beaten body into any seasons past those at Azusa. As a result, when the league folded surprisingly during my senior season, it seemed like just another item in the news to me. On the other hand, when guys started dropping onto the locker room benches with dazed looks and their heads in their hands to the refrain of, "what am I going to do now?" I found myself starting to freak out as well. What was I going to do now?

Other than that looming mental melt-down, things were going well for me. I'd picked up a couple brochures and course catalogs for graduate schools, because I had been toying with the idea of becoming a lawyer or a minister. On most days, I found that I was leaning toward the law, but then I would swing back toward the church. The one thing of which I was certain was that my girlfriend of the last six months, Melanie, was going to be a part of whatever I did next.

By the end of my senior season, Melanie's charms and Azusa's decidedly pro-marriage philosophy had worked their magic—I decided I was going to propose. Having no money in the bank (I was hardly able to get by on the $25 from my step-grandma as it was), I began looking for alternatives to a traditional engagement ring. Pawn shops quickly proved too expensive (and the thought of buying someone else's dream on the cheap felt too weird), and a check-in with my mom suggested that there were no family rings I could use. Discouraged, I did what any emotional eater would do—I turned to candy. In this case, it was a gumball machine, and it was ripe for the spare nickel I had in my pocket. The machine was paired with an identical twin that carried trinkets inside plastic bubbles. Near the top, I noticed that inside one of the transparent balls was a ring that read "LOVE" with a fake diamond inside the "O." No one would mistake the ring as real. You could see the seam where the plastic mold pressed together. I took it as a sign, however. Standing in front of that toy machine, I closed my eyes and prayed that my nickel would bring me that cheesy little ring.

It did.

I proposed the next day.

She said yes.

And, I still didn't know what I was going to do after college.

I decided that I'd best meet with a counselor to plan for my suddenly adjusted priorities. He informed me that while I was perfectly positioned academically for either law school or the seminary, neither one of them would lead me to much of an income any time soon. I asked him what I could do that was fast. He said I could teach. That statement triggered a memory—Fred Mangini, the vice principal who was in charge of the "Cool It Squad," had told me that if I ever got my teaching credential, he'd hire me. I pictured going back and teaching at Carlmont, living in a house on the hill with Melanie and a kid or two. I told the counselor I was sold.

Finding a situation that matched my financial status as a no-no (no money saved and no money earned) should have been difficult. Apparently, however, somebody somewhere liked me enough to let it all work out. While I was going to get my teaching credential through Azusa, I was going to be taking my classes at the college of Notre Dame in the Bay Area, while living for free at Menlo in exchange for coaching at their high school. Melanie was going to come with me, even though she still had a year of school left. Our plan was for her to work to help us find a way to purchase frivolous things, like food. It seemed like we'd found a way to make my additional semester of school pay for itself. By the time I was finished, however, it was the prospect of getting paid to teach that looked bleak.

✦ ✦ ✦

I entered the field of teaching at the worst possible time in California. There were rumblings that in the mid-term elections of 1978, there was going to be a ballot measure to cap property taxes. While the proponents of the measure championed the dollars that were going to be staying in the homeowners' pockets, everyone in education was aware that those were dollars that would have come their way. Unfortunately, nobody told the blissfully ignorant and recently married me that my little plan might not be tailor-made for the current economic climate. So, when I entered the teaching program, everyone said I should go into special education, where there was always a need for teachers. I could have very easily listened to them. Undoubtedly, it would have been hard to deny the guy with no hands and a teaching credential the opportunity to teach disabled students. But, that wasn't where my heart was. I wanted to teach social studies, the least desirable credential in any job market. Nobody has ever said my game plans are flawless.

Thankfully, once I got started, I found out that my Azusa financial aid was going to cover the cost of tuition (I like to think I do a better job of keeping tabs on my players' financial aid than I did my own). As a result, all I had to worry about was finishing the program and finding a job. In six months, I had achieved the first objective; the next Monday, I achieved the second.

Apparently, Fred Mangini had been keeping his eye on me, because as soon as my name showed up on the substitute manifest for his new school, Menlo-Atherton, he gave me a call. Coincidentally, they needed a full-time sub in special ed to cover the rest of the year, and Mangini had me pegged for it. For the first time, I was going to be making money, not shilling it out. All that stood between me and the job were some paperwork and fingerprints.

When I showed up at the district office, I was more than a little bit nervous. I'd heard horror stories about contentious meetings and arguments about the most mundane of administrative forms, as well as about the manhandling classmates had received while having their fingers rolled across the ink pad and paper. I had no idea how they would handle my single digits, considering their five squares, even though I thought they might just have me blot in compass points of my wrist in the first four and an impression of the middle in the fifth. Five unidentifiable blobs in order to identify the one guy with no hands. I imagine that it would seem sound to a bureaucrat.

While I was finishing my deranged daydream, I was called back to a small cubicle. The administrative assistant invited me to sit, and asked if I had my paperwork. I presented it to her, and we went through each document to ensure it was properly filled out. The conversation was both professional and cordial. By the end of the meeting, I was officially a substitute for the second semester at my old high school—without an inkpad being taken out or a word being spoken about a fingerprint.

That semester was a whirlwind. I'd had no training whatsoever in special education. Similar as with everyone else, I was expected to do something extra. As a result, I was a track coach. To think that my first job was teaching in the class that I'd fought my entire life to stay out of and coaching the last sport that the podiatrists ever thought I'd ever be a part of is one of life's little ironies that seem set up to test my mettle. Somehow I survived, even though I was certain that I didn't want to teach special education for the rest of my life, and that there were not going to be jobs at Menlo-Atherton in social studies the next year. Accordingly, I'd have to strike out on my own to find a job.

My first hope was that Fred Mangini was going to be able to hire me at his new school, San Carlos. He anticipated this possibility and preemptively called to let me know there weren't going to be any jobs at his school, nor were there going to be any much of anywhere—the ballot measure capping property taxes had passed.

I was beginning to get nervous. Melanie was only employed part-time, and with the entire economy in the middle of what the newspapers were calling "stagflation," we needed to just be happy if she had any kind of job. There started to be a rumor going around that one district had somehow managed to pass a levy that was going to pay to open a new school—North Monterey County High. Furthermore, they were going to have to hire an entire staff. It seemed as if everyone in the state was talking about North Monterey as the refuge for the teachers who had lost their jobs due to budget cuts. Knowing full well that it was going to be an exercise in futility, I applied to North Monterey.

Several weeks after I had submitted my application, as well as after days of mentally preparing myself to hit the pavement looking for anyone who would hire me, I received a call informing me that North Monterey High School wanted to interview me for a position. I had my foot in the door. Now, I just had to figure out what I was supposed to do when I got there. I'd never been through a job interview in my life.

I knew that you were supposed to look good for an interview. So, I had Melanie button my top button and clip on my best (and only) tie over the collared shirt that I'd worn to concerts at Azusa. I didn't own a jacket, but Melanie assured me I looked professional enough for a teacher. As far as either one of us knew, I was as ready as I could be.

❖ ❖ ❖

I'd put on my application that I could coach anything—football, soccer, baseball, track—and that I was credentialed in social studies. It was the most trite combination outside of the PE teacher/coach, and I wondered how I would stand out from any of the veteran candidates from nearby Salinas, who had been the hardest hit by both the budget cuts and the opening of the new school. I worried that maybe they had just put me on the manifest for show. Or worse, I began to think that Fred Mangini had put in a good word for me, and that now I had to perform well for him.

By the time I walked into that conference room, I felt as if I had just played a football game. When I saw all the people seated around the table, I thought I was going to have to play another. At the head of the table, was a guy dressed in a shiny suit and sunglasses. Today, he would pass for a sports agent. On that day, he was the principal of the school. He was flanked by the superintendent, the assistant superintendent, the assistant principal, every department head, two community members, and two students. They all had the confidence that comes from having the power in the room. They were well aware of the fact that they were the only school in the state that was hiring and that every teacher who walked through that door was desperate for a job. There I was, sitting at the end of the table, with a clip-on tie.

"So, Mark, do you have any experience?"

Apparently, the interview was beginning. So, I answered honestly, explaining that I had just graduated and that I had taught special education for a semester at Menlo-Atherton High School.

"But, you are applying for a social studies position, correct?"

I explained that I had been a substitute in the special education class, but that my credential was in social studies. I told them that history and government were passions for me, and that I had contemplated going to law school before deciding on becoming a teacher. Several of the people at the table nodded at this.

"Besides being someone who wants to teach social studies, tell us a little more about yourself."

I told them about growing up in the Bay Area and how both coaches and teachers had changed my life. As I was telling the stories, I could see smiles cropping up around the room, and I began to feel more at ease.

"Why do you want this job?"

My instinct was to say that it was the only one in the state, but I was able to avoid that answer, and I segued into the one I'd thought about on the drive over. I was effusive in my praise of North Monterey as a place where my wife and I could start a family, and excited about the opportunity to create traditions at this new, state-of-the-art high school. The panel seemed to be hanging on my every word.

As the questioning continued, I began to think, *I'm doing it! There are no boundaries! I truly can be all that I can be.* Based on this overwhelming response to me and my story, I wondered if rather than simply being offered the job if it was going to come with some sort of coronation. The parade would run down main street, I would be on the last float, giving new meaning to the phrase "elbow-elbow, wrist-wrist" and—

"Mark, the chair of our social studies department would like you to answer some questions now."

Torn from my reverie, I realized that the panel had subsequently turned toward one of their own. The object of their apparent affection sat poised in his chair, with one hand massaging his manicured goatee. His bent arm exposed the dark brown elbow patch on his light tweed jacket, and at that moment, I knew the interview was going to take some sort of turn.

"Mr. Speckman," the man took his hand off his beard and placed it slowly on the table, "To what social studies theorist do you most closely align your teaching style?"

< Cough, cough! >

I half-choked on my own saliva only to have all of it vanish a moment later. *What the hell had that guy asked?* I remembered that someone had told me in an elementary school spelling bee that if you weren't sure about how to spell the word to ask them to repeat it.

"Sorry about that...had a little coughing fit. Could you please repeat the question?"

The social studies chair cleared his throat. "To what social studies theorist do you most closely align your teaching style?"

"Well..." I wanted to backpedal, to digress more into my life story, which seemed to have so captivated my audience. At this point, however, they seemed to be hanging on to professor perfect goatee's every word. Besides, linebackers are taught never to backpedal. The thought of thousands of teachers without jobs flashed through my mind. I imagined a breadline dedicated to teachers, with its entrants passing the time, as they waited for their stale portions by thumbing through district catalogues, ready to jump at the most remedial of positions. I was at the back of that line, and they were out of catalogues. I shook the thought and figured that if I didn't say something intelligible in the next three seconds I had better start for the breadline. I knew that I needed a name, and I needed a theory if I wanted this job. So, I synthesized the first educational name with the first football coaching technique that came into my mind.

"The theorist that I keep coming back to is Fred Mangini, the author of the Mangini theory, which we all know is whole-part-whole."

The nods and smiles returned to people's faces.

"Oh, yes, the Mangini theory," professor goatee said through pursed lips, "can you tell us a bit more about it?"

"The purpose behind the concept of whole-part-whole…" I started rattling off coach-speak with social studies ideas and made sure to drop in my old vice principal's name periodically to validate my response. By the end of my answer, even I was starting to believe that the Mangini theory would work well in a social studies classroom. In the process, the panel started to glow again. Buoyed by their support, I began to elaborate on its success in both rural and urban settings, from the largest schools down to the smallest. By the end of my answer, I was pretty sure that the parade was back on.

"Well Mr. Speckman," the professor made eye contact with me, and we each were certain the other man was the biggest liar in the room, "I can tell you that I think we are all subscribers of the Mangini theory."

"We certainly are," intoned the principal. "Now, we've got one last portion of the interview to conduct, but that will be completed by the head football coach alone. So, if you don't have any questions for us, I would be glad to take you down to meet him."

As long as he didn't ask any more questions about the Mangini theory, I didn't have any questions for him.

The football coach was down in an office below the gym. His door was shut, but I could see through the window that his desk was a mess of papers and brochures, while a meticulously organized shelf of game film was over his shoulder. The superintendent knocked, and after a moment, we watched the coach wheel himself over to the door and open it.

"Yeah?"

"Coach, I would like to introduce Mark—"

"Hey," a kid's head appeared between the superintendent's shoulder and my own, "does anybody know first aid?"

The coach hopped out of his seat, filled a bag of ice, and started out of the locker room. Knowing that all that stood between me and a job was my interview with him, I followed.

By the time we got up to the injury, I was completely unaware of my surroundings. It wasn't until I saw the grimace on the patient's face that I realized that it was the vice principal and that we were back in the interview room. He apparently had wrenched his knee standing up to leave, and the small crowd that huddled around the victim was made up of the same faces as my interview had been.

The coach looked at me before applying the bag of ice to the vice principal's injured knee, which caused everyone in the crowd look at me. *Were they testing me again? Was this my second panel interview? Did they think I was an expert in something other than the Mangini theory?*

Not knowing what else to say, I stated tentatively, "Maybe we should immobilize it."

At this counsel, everyone nodded. I held the knee in place, while the coach ran off to grab some splints. I looked up at the principal. He smiled, put his sunglasses back over his eyes, and disappeared from the room.

I found out the next week that I was one of only two new teachers that had been hired for the 35 open positions.

On the other hand, I didn't get a parade.

Chapter 12 This Is What You Call Gainful Employment?

For the first time, I was without financial aid. Not only was I on my own two feet, supporting my wife, buying a house ... and I didn't even have a place to work. Because North Monterey County High School's construction had run into delays, it wasn't slated to open until October 28. In other words, not only did I not have a classroom (or much of a paycheck), but the team didn't have a field. We found a refuge at the local elementary school and established a locker room in the garden shed (we used to joke that while the University of Georgia may play between the hedges, we got dressed between the hedge trimmers).

I was the head freshman coach. Technically, it was a freshman-sophomore team, but it was decided that, as a team without seniors, we would play a full varsity schedule with sophomores and juniors. In other words, we were the last group that got to use the shed, and always we got the roughest patch of grass on the miniscule field.

My less-than-desirable situation was not helped by our head coach who had determined that I was officially an idiot. As a 23-year-old just out of teaching school, I was hardly positioned to argue with the man. He must have simply divined it, because he barely had the time to call me an idiot, much less establish my credibility as one. For my part, I didn't think much of him either. He had made a concerted effort in our first coaches' meeting that he was not to be questioned, that we were going to win, regardless of the cost, and that regardless of one's (or his) marital status, women were going to be hit on. The only support I ever received from the guy was a playbook that I was expected to run without further explanation.

Even as a coaching neophyte, I had a feeling it was going to be one of those seasons.

Boy, was I right.

By the time the first game rolled around, I felt like I had the freshman playing as well as a guy learning the offense and defense from a piece of paper could. We were playing another freshman-only team. Fortunately, my instincts about the team were right—we walked away with the win. The varsity's fortune was not so kind—they endured a 49-0 drubbing. On the other hand, I was feeling good about what my little freshmen had accomplished.

Over the next two weeks, we reeled off a pair of wins, and I'd managed a makeover for our house's bathroom. At 3-0 going into October with a wife who was happy to be able to take baths in her redone powder room, I figured I couldn't have asked for a better start to my first school year.

Then, as if I was a character in a Hemingway novel, the first cold front of the fall rolled into the bay. The torrential downpour it delivered had rain coming into the house sideways. After a quick (and wet) investigation, I discovered it was the gravel-tar roof that was leaking, and I gave myself a crash-course in roofing. A bit of research established asphalt shingles as the best option. So, I set out to have the roof gravel shoveled off by the next day (Sunday).

I don't recall ever working as hard as I did that Saturday, but somehow I managed to get that entire roof cleaned off and tarped over, so that it was ready for shingles the next day (looking back, I realize it was a really small house). I had no delusions. I was aware that hammering took me a bit longer than the average guy. On the other hand, with fall apparently in full swing, I knew I needed to get that roof finished as fast as possible. Accordingly, I set out for what I was certain was going to be another 12-hour day on that roof. Less than two hours into the project, however, Melanie came out to tell me the principal was on the phone. Dropping my shingles, I made my way down the ladder and into the house.

"Yes?" I managed between breaths.

"We need you to come down to the district office."

For what? I thought. "I'm kind of busy. My roof—"

"We need to know what you know."

"What I know?"

"Mark," the principal's voice lowered, "come down to the district office."

"Okay."

I didn't know why, but the roof would have to wait.

When I got down to the district office and saw the looks on people's faces, the altar boy in me immediately thought wake. By the time the principal and superintendent sat me down, I was fairly certain there was no dead body in the room, but I still wondered if there was one nearby.

"Did you have anything to do with the eligibility?" asked one of them.

"What eligibility?"

"What do you know about it?" fired off the other.

"I, uh, what are we talking about?"

After several different permutations of the same questions, my utter ignorance seemed to garner their trust, and they informed me what was happening. Apparently, the coaches on staff had been in collusion to get some players eligible by having them take correspondence classes over the summer, with some anonymous students performing the coursework for them. (As the story was told to me, I was able to fill in some mental gaps as I recalled that in one of our first meetings the head coach asking if I'd hung onto any of my term papers and if he could see them.) For these transgressions, the entire varsity staff was being suspended for three weeks, with the head coach and his top assistant suspended for the entire season.

"Wow." I was shocked. "What are we going to do with the football team?"

"Well," the principal and superintendent looked at each other, "this situation is going to hit the newspapers tomorrow, and in them, you are going to be announced as our interim head coach."

Frankly, I didn't know how to respond. In reality, I said the first thing that came to my head. "We should cancel the varsity season and put the sophomores down on the frosh-soph team. We only have 16 juniors. That would help build the program."

The answer came immediately, as if my idea had been anticipated. "No, you can't do that."

"Oh. Then, what are we going to do?"

At 23 years old, I became not only the head of a football program, but the head coach of both teams.

◆ ◆ ◆

My two assistants and I didn't have enough experience to try to change the culture of the team. Furthermore, even if we had, there were barely enough of us to manage a practice, much less develop a new mindset. Each day became about survival, and that was never more evident than on game day.

In California back then, the frosh-soph and varsity games were played back-to-back on Fridays. As a rule, most varsity coaches had a built-in routine that included meals, walkthroughs, and warm-ups. This ritual inevitably included the head coach—except on my team. With three guys on staff, we were left to simply "encourage" the varsity players to come watch the frosh-soph game after they'd managed to get a meal in their stomachs. At the end of the third quarter, my two assistants left to get the varsity warmed up and ready for their game, while I coached our freshman team by myself. When the gun sounded, it may have meant the end of the game for those freshmen, but it signaled the start of the second half of my marathon evening.

Oftentimes in football, a player or a team can get its second wind from the fans. At the end of that first game, I was desperately in need of that kind of push. On the other hand, I certainly wasn't going to be getting it from our crowd. Since our coach—a guy who had been recruited from Southern California to open the school's program—had been suspended, it looked like our fans had suffered the same fate. It was like a ghost town up in the stands. I can't say they were missing much. We got drilled every time we stepped on the field. In reality, however, it definitely helped to have the bleachers clear so that I could see when one of the freshmen who was supposed to be under my supervision had begun to wander around the stadium during the varsity game.

After one of my six varsity debacles, a local newspaper reporter asked me how I felt. I told him the truth: I was tired. Before the issue could have hit half the newsstands, the principal was in my classroom (the school had finally opened).

"You can't say you're tired."

I tried to explain that I hadn't meant that I was tired of losing, or that I was tired of having to run two teams, or that I was tired of not having headphones since the old head coach had refused to relinquish them, but simply that I was tired from five hours of coaching a game that I was passionate about.

"Still, you can't say you're tired."

So, I didn't for the rest of our totally defeated season.

Besides, by that time, I was too tired to speak anyway.

Chapter 13 So That's It … I'm a Football Coach

As hard as my first season at North Monterey County was, and as ready as I was for it to end, within a week I was ready to do it all over again. You could call it youthful exuberance, blissful ignorance, or a latent masochistic tendency, but something had changed within me during those two months. There was something exciting about working with a group of young men and striving to achieve something bigger than any of us could fathom.

We were Sisyphus that season, and while the rock was too big to move very far (and when we did, it always seemed to roll back over us on the way down), each attempt brought us closer together. We had our own brand of gallows humor. Given our designation as the NMC Condors, I would joke in staff meetings that we were circling ourselves. Furthermore, we entered the "Con-dome" (my name for the stadium) each week, certain we had done everything we could to avoid a 49-0 shellacking. I am still in contact with some of the guys from that first team I coached. To a man, they tell me that it was one of the best experiences of their life. While I didn't enjoy it at the time, it is one the most vivid seasons in my memory, and I look back on it fondly. I can also tell you that we never lost a game 49-0 under my watch.

Not ever losing by seven touchdowns doesn't sound like much of a rallying cry, but when the district posted the head-coaching position as open for the next season, I submitted my name. When my predecessor submitted his name, I championed the fact I had never lost a game as badly as he did. In my mind, I had taken over a program in disarray, and had been asked to do more with less than any coach in the district. Furthermore, I had somehow managed to provide an experience everyone would remember. To me, I should have been the leader in the clubhouse, and based on my previous success interviewing with the school, a shoe-in for the job.

I was not given the position.

At the time, I was pissed. Who were they to turn their backs on the guy who salvaged the season? Today, I couldn't be more thankful that they gave the job to Phil Maas and Roger Sugimoto. I was too young and precocious to see that there was still quite a bit that I needed to learn before I would be able to become the kind of coach I wanted to be. Also, who would've guessed that the thing I would learn in my second season of coaching would be the "fly," the play that has become the signature of my offenses?

◆ ◆ ◆

When the next season started, Phil Maas took me under his wing. Everything that he wanted to do, he ran by all of the assistants, whether we had been under him before or not. He wanted our input. As a result, we discussed what he wanted to install as our offensive and defensive schemes. As a linebacker, I could see the rationale behind a variety of defensive schemes. As a consequence, convincing me what we were going to run wasn't that difficult. Just so long as it appeared sound to my eye, I was on-board.

Offensively, however, I was a bit of a neophyte. My entire experience came from a season of running plays from a suspended coach's playbook. I found myself needing more explanations for everything, since it was so new to me, and I was so predisposed to asking questions. Fortunately, Phil informed us he was going to run the veer, an offense with which I was intimately familiar from playing against it. It is also an offense that, at least in meetings and on chalkboards, is quite simple.

The veer is an offense in which you don't have to have the best athletes to succeed, just the best discipline. Having coached the entire team the previous year, I knew that having an offense that required something other than great athletes was of paramount importance. Not surprisingly, they heard no arguments from me … not until Phil mentioned "the other thing" he wanted to run.

As all coaches do when introducing a new scheme, Phil went to the chalkboard and began drawing Xs and Os. Pre-snap motion is typically drawn with a squiggly line. As a result, when Phil started drawing the motion, I figured it would fall into one of the two categories that I'd seen. It would either be short motion, in which a receiver stays on his side of the field, a move typically designed to give him a head start on an assignment or pass route, or long motion across the formation, in which the quarterback is able to discern whether the defense is in a man or a zone. When Phil's squiggly line continued on into the lineman, I was certain that I was going to be seeing the latter. Instead, the squiggly line then stopped—right behind the quarterback.

By his very positioning, this player had lost his effectiveness as a receiver. This player was also too small to act as much of a lead blocker. Furthermore, he was too close to the quarterback to take a handoff going anywhere. In addition, because he was aligned directly behind the center and guard, he wouldn't have any time to build up the momentum that would be necessary to plunge into some tiny hole.

" … and when the guy gets right here," Phil pointed at the very spot where I was looking, "we will snap it and hand him the ball."

Phil then proceeded to color that player's circle in (meaning he was getting the ball), and drew a straight line that continued to be parallel to the line of scrimmage, until it was well clear of the tackle.

"So, you're going to hand the ball to a guy who is running toward the sideline?" I was more than skeptical. As a defensive guy, getting the offense to run east and west, as opposed to north and south, was what we strived for, and our offense was going to do this *on purpose?*

Phil said yes, and continued drawing on the board, explaining why he thought it would work. Currently, he emphasized that it was only going to be a part of our offense, not the whole thing. Phil's explanation assuaged some of my doubts. It would be hard to lose yards going sideways. Furthermore, if we only ran it a few times a game, maybe we'd surprise the defense and pick up a yard or two. On the other hand, it was the veer offense that I believed in, and I figured that by mid-season, we'd be a veer-only team.

I was half-right.

During that season, I watched as we toiled away at the veer, working on the mesh between the fullback and the quarterback, working on the down blocks of the guards and tackles, and working on the pitch relationship between the quarterback and the tailback. In the process, we achieved a moderate level of success. I also watched as the 5 to 10 minutes we'd spend our gadget play, which Phil called "the fly sweep," and saw that every time we ran it, we would pick up eight or nine yards and on occasion, break a big one.

Our ability to gain yardage when employing the fly didn't mean we ran it more often—we all thought that the fly's success as a change of pace play—but I began to believe in it and to wonder about its potential for growth. Phil must have too, because he built in some plays where we faked the hand-off to the "sweeper" and either gave to a player up the middle or passed off of it. On the other hand, we only ran the fly out of one formation. We were going to be a veer team, come hell or high water.

After that season, I was starting to get growing pains. I had learned a ton under Phil and Roger, but I was ready to move on. I don't know if it was the fact that I had the opportunity to be a head coach that had affected my perception of the normal promotion rate for coaches. It could also have been that I missed the Bay Area, or if Melanie's pregnancy had resulted in me wanting to be closer to my own mom. The point is that when an opening to be the defensive coordinator for the exclusive Menlo college preparatory high school team, as well as a P.E. teacher occurred, I jumped at it.

I think Melanie was excited about the move too. She quickly landed a job, and we realized that with free campus housing, we had a chance to save some money to eventually buy our own house. All of which didn't mean there weren't some changes to my normal routine.

Even in just two years at North Monterey County High School, I'd become accustomed to teaching history to a full class of students from different backgrounds. At Menlo, I was teaching physical education to classes of twelve, eight, and two, comprised of children from extremely wealthy families. To my students, I was the lowest form of academic life—a requisite hurdle in their rite of passage toward a Stanford or Ivy League education. I was eating lunch with the students which, although invigorating, reminded me that I was living in a two-bedroom apartment with a pregnant wife, on a high school and college campus. On the field, I was coordinating a defense with complete autonomy, and I was working under the nicest guy that I could have imagined. I could also see that he wasn't as into it as much as I was. In my eyes, it was as if Menlo was a rite of passage on my way to running my own program.

❖ ❖ ❖

At about this same time, a good friend of mine, Don Brock, told me that I needed to start looking at the Valley. The San Joaquin region was just starting to boom. It had a ton of jobs, as well as cheap real estate, which was the perfect combination for a new father wanting to provide for his family. I figured I would apply for every head coaching position that was open in the Valley, certain I was going to land one of them.

I couldn't even get an interview.

Confident that I just needed a chance to sell myself in person, as opposed to on paper, I hand delivered my very thin resume to Livingston High School's principal. Our conversation was brief, and I figured that it would again come down to the words that I had typed on a page. At that point, I began preparing for my next round of applications.

When I got the call from Livingston for an interview, I was surprised. I then prepped as if I was going to be facing the same panel that I had at North Monterey County High School. By that time, I had even managed to develop some personal anecdotes involving the Mangini method. Subsequently, my interview at Livingston went similar to how the one at North Monterey had. I got to talk about things in which I was confident—e.g., my background, why I liked to teach and coach, etc. I even got a question that I didn't know exactly how to answer. This time, however, the difficult question wasn't about social studies pedagogy from an uppity guy in a tweed jacket. Rather, it involved a regular-looking guy wondering how I was going to use keys.

I remember looking at the questioner and the rest of the panel before answering. I couldn't tell if they were serious or joking. *Well, like I did at my last job, I take the key chain out of my pocket, find the key I need, stick it in the lock, turn it, and the door just seems to open for me. I do something pretty similar when I go to start my car or even enter my home. Amazingly, it seems to work in those places as well—is that how it works here?*

"Mark, you don't have to answer that," said Bill Elam, Livingston's principal.

"Oh, okay." I remembered being a little bit disappointed that I didn't get to answer the question.

Just like my interview with North Monterey, I felt confident that I was going to get the job ... and I did, after the high school's first choice turned down the offer.

Melanie, Tim, and I were headed for Livingston.

◆ ◆ ◆

It was obvious from the beginning that Bill Elam believed in me (and for that I will be forever thankful). Looking back, however, I'm not quite sure why he did. I had very little experience. This was going to be my fourth year as a coach and my second as a head coach. In reality, my time at helm of North Monterey must have read like "took over as captain, after the Titanic hit the iceberg." All I had was enthusiasm. Furthermore, as the head football coach, head soccer coach, and band advisor, I was going to need it.

When I began to meet with my football staff, it became apparent that Livingston had no real football tradition. They weren't a team that parents, faculty, and fans expected to run the option or the wishbone. They also weren't a team expected to make deep runs into the playoffs, or even make the playoffs at all. As such, the Livingston football program was looking for something, anything, on which they could hang their hats. As the guy who was going to be calling the shots for the first time on offense, I decided that we'd try something new, something different, as the basis of our offense. We would hang our hats on the fly sweep.

What I didn't realize then was that I'd still be hanging my hat on that play over 30 years later.

With the fly being nothing more than a series of four plays out of one formation when I left North Monterey, I knew that some work had to be done with it to make it the basis for an offense. I remembered Phil Maas' attention to the detail of the mesh point on the veer and the importance of carrying out the fakes whether you had the ball or not. I figured that I could apply that same degree of refinement to the fly.

Subsequently, I devoted several periods of practice to the fakes that each potential ballcarrier would be performing. Like Phil, I heavily emphasized the importance of the quarterback's role in what seemed like a fly/full/tailback-heavy offense. I even appropriated the term "mesh" from the veer. Similar to what we had done at North Monterey, the offensive line had less emphasis on manhandling guys and more on shielding defenders from the man with the ball. It was as if we were running the veer offense on the fly.

Our first season was one of moderate success in terms of our record (5-4). On the other hand, it felt absolutely triumphant to the players and their parents. I wasn't quite so easy to please. While we had come a long way that season, I knew that we were still just scratching the surface. By focusing so much on fundamentals that first year, the playbook had only grown by a play. As such, we were still a one-formation team. In the off-season, I began looking for ways to have us run the same plays in the same ways, but make them look different to the opponent. With a season of running the plays we already had under our belts, I wanted to add a few plays to our playbook. After a summer of toiling away, our playbook had nearly doubled in size, weighing in at a whopping eight plays out of two different formations. (Hey, we've all got to start somewhere.)

When the next season got underway, I was amazed by how much our kids had grown as players. The linemen were recognizing defensive fronts faster and adjusting the blocking patterns that we'd used the previous week—or even the previous season—if necessary. The backs were finding new holes in the defenses that were created by those adjusted schemes. I was also growing as a coach. For example, I began to recognize not only how defenses were gearing up to stop us, but the creases and seams they were vacating. Overpursuit by the defense spawned the red-light sweep (where the player in fly-motion takes the ball, giving every indication to the defense that he's heading wide, before he cuts inside behind the linemen who were sealing everyone to the outside). My realization that the league powerhouse, Central Catholic, was using the fullback to key in to the direction of each play triggered my development of false keys. Even our mistakes were serendipitous. Our QB keeper play was created, when our QB broke his hand and had trouble throwing the ball. It seemed like everything we did worked. In reality, with no preconceived notions about how offense should work, thinking outside the box wasn't a problem. Furthermore, to begin with, I didn't even have a box.

After each discovery, however, I would call Phil Maas and ask him what he thought. He would usually tell me, "What the hell? Why not try it?" So, I would. By the end of the season, I had developed a series of plays that I wanted to run so that I could see how each defense was going to respond. I felt like an offensive genius (until I subsequently found out that Bill Walsh had been doing it for 10 years).

As such, it felt like we were having the kind of season where everything was going to go our way. We had managed to tie for the league championship with Central Catholic by splitting our two games with them. We were also facing a coin flip to determine which of us was going to get to represent our conference in the sectional playoffs.

I was certain our luck was going to continue, as I drove into the parking lot where the coin flip was to be held. There was no way it couldn't. We were too good a story to be denied. When I found the lamppost in the parking lot where the league president was waiting, I pulled up and climbed out of the car. I had come to this halfway point alone and had assumed that the Central Catholic coach would do the same. I was surprised when three silhouettes stepped from another vehicle. The first one to step into the light was the coach followed by his eight-year-old son. Had my son Tim been eight, I would have done the same thing. The third figure was a priest. I knew we were in trouble.

The league president brought out a quarter, asked what Central Catholic wanted to call (I think the league president felt that they had the divine right to call it), and the coach said heads. The quarter bounced on the ground twice and rolled under the Central Catholic coach's car. His son dove in after it, and started screaming, "It's heads! It's heads!" before he'd even gotten out from under the vehicle.

I had instinctively started walking to my car before the quarter had even hit the asphalt and had to jog back to shake the president's, coach's, and priest's hands, before I began the long drive back home alone.

Little did I know that that would be the first of many long drives that I would do alone.

Or, that would be my last act as Livingston's head football coach.

God works in mysterious ways.

Chapter 14 Welcome to the Big Time (in California)

It never ceases to amaze me how far coaches will go to get the slightest edge. For years, I've gone to colleges up and down the West Coast. I've attended the Nike coaches' clinic in Portland. I've flown to the American Football Coaches Association conferences on numerous occasions. Frankly, I've never come away with a new offense, a new defense, or even a new coach. On the other hand, every year, so long as I can say I've learned at least one thing that can improve my program—be it a fundamental, a scheme, a recruiting tactic, or even an administrative duty, my efforts were undoubtedly a success. After my second year at Livingston, my classroom became a place where some coaches from other schools came to get their edge for the next year.

There were coaches from small schools and big schools, as well as schools from up north and down south. In reality, I have to admit that it felt good to have put a program on the map. As more and more coaches rolled in with their staffs, however, the more I realized that Livingston was always going to be a school of 500 kids, that I was always going to be coaching two sports, and that I was never going to be able to create the kind of football culture I had grown up to crave. Looking back, I don't know why I felt I had to leave Livingston. Bill Elam was an amazing principal, the kids' commitment in the class and on the field was unparalleled, and I couldn't have asked for a more appreciative community. On the other hand, I was young, a bit precocious, and ready to test myself at the next level. A job offer in Gilroy provided me with the opportunity; I wish, however, I'd have known what that test would entail before I consented to take it.

◆ ◆ ◆

Gilroy seemed like it would be a good fit for both me and my family. It was a one-school town, which meant a lot for me professionally. It meant that everyone on the street would be supporting us both emotionally and (hopefully) financially, as opposed to one of our rivals. It also meant that, as chronic underachievers, that I might be given the latitude to do things differently than they'd been done in the past, since everyone was so starved for a winner. More importantly, the schools in Gilroy were known for their quality, and with Tim about to turn four, Melanie and I thought everything about the decision was easy—except for the fact that we weren't going to be able to afford to buy a house in Gilroy. Having been raised to believe that real estate was the world's safest investment, we decided I'd commute for the first year and lease a place in Gilroy and rent out our house in North Monterey County the second year. That way, we'd have somewhere to call home, should our move to Gilroy not go as planned.

Once I had the job in Gilroy and had resigned my position at Livingston, I would make periodic trips down to meet with the staff. My first few meetings were to introduce myself and the fly offense. It quickly became apparent that Gilroy's staff had not been one of those who had come up to Livingston to learn the virtues of the fly. They were asking the same questions that I'd asked three years before. To the extent possible, I did everything that I could to assuage their concerns, just as Phil had done for me, using chalk, anecdotes, and film from our past two seasons.

The only difference was that when Phil showed up at North Monterey, it was the second year the school had been in existence. Furthermore, it was my third year coaching. I didn't know any better. Gilroy had been around for over 50 years and had been running the I-formation for nearly as long, with a group of veteran coaches who had never thought about doing anything differently. At the end of our third meeting, I'm pretty sure that I had them convinced that I was a cocky young coach, with an offense from a small school who was going to run the fly come hell or high water. Fortunately, they seemed willing to give it a try.

Having the offense somewhat settled, the next time I drove down to Gilroy, it was to talk about defense. I had arranged to meet Vern Kellerman, the previous season's defensive coordinator, in his classroom at 3:30 to see what his thoughts were about the upcoming season. He knew that I'd called both sides of the ball at Livingston. I was concerned that he would enter our meeting with the wrong type of attitude about his position on the staff. What transpired, however, was likely the longest conversation ever held about whether it was possible to stop an out in the 4-4 defense. At one o'clock the next morning, I left his classroom, convinced that not only could you stop the out from a 4-4 defense, but that Vern Kellerman was the guy to make sure that it happened.

Having found someone who was a better defensive coach than I'd ever be was a relief. As a result, I would now be able to focus entirely on the coaching the offense. Furthermore, with a vibrant athletic director and a gifted staff, I felt like I could be the kind of coach that I wanted to be. I was able to develop more plays out of more formations and to build a cohesive program, from the middle schools on up. We were able to hold clinics for the Pop Warner coaches about what offense we'd run when the kids got to the high school, as well as how to teach the fundamentals that would prepare them for the future. I was certain I could turn Gilroy into a powerhouse.

Then, the season started. Plays that should have worked didn't, and mistakes that shouldn't have happened did. In the last game of the year, we finally put it all together and won … our only victory of the year. 1-8-1 was not the mark of an up-and-coming team, and having an article in the paper about your offense entitled, "Fly or Folly?" was not the mark of an up-and-coming coach. Coaches from around our league were quoted as saying the fly was nothing special, and was quite easy to stop.

That particular journalist's sentiments were echoed by people on the street, and as someone who is virtually incapable of disguising his identity, I heard my fair share of catcalls. I didn't know for sure, but I was fairly confident that this wasn't what Gilroy had expected when they hired me. I was certain that it wasn't what Melanie and Tim had signed on for.

When the season was over, I took some time to reflect on what had seemed like an awful year. Although I like to think of myself as a perpetual optimist, that season introduced me to the concept of self-doubt. Could the fly work at such a big school? Was I ready to run a program the size of Gilroy? Perhaps more importantly, how big a mistake had it been to leave Livingston? It was beginning to seem like the only good decision that I'd made in the past six months was to keep the house up in North Monterey. Even if we had moved back to North Monterey, I didn't know if I could legally evict the current occupants on the grounds of my team's poor play.

Sensing myself beginning to spiral, I began to watch film, in an attempt to let my miserable memories commiserate with the reality of our poor play. A funny thing happened on my way to football melancholy; however, I realized that we were a lot better than I thought. We weren't missing making plays by yards, or even feet, but by inches. Holes were showing up on film that I didn't see in the heat of the game. Our players' eyes just weren't ready to see them. Blocks that I hadn't thought were made had been. They just weren't being held long enough. I was reminded of something Coach Solari had once told me. On film, you never look as good or as bad as you thought that you did during the game. We were an offense on the brink of something big, and nobody seemed to know it.

Buoyed by my revelations, I began post-season meetings with my players and coaches. Almost to a man, while the players were disappointed about our record, they had cherished the experience and thanked me for a great season. My assistant coaches concurred, with each reminding me that Gilroy had only been to the playoffs once in the previous 20 years. Furthermore, each assistant was certain that with another year under our belts, we might just make it two for 21. Galvanized, the players, coaches, and I launched into our off-season program, working to develop more strength, faster speed, and an enhanced level of awareness of how big the little things can truly be.

The next year, we managed to finish 6-4, barely missing the playoffs, and setting the stage for a miracle run the following year. Our efforts also helped ensure that there were not going to be articles written about the folly of the fly offense this off-season.

In 1985, my third year at Gilroy, we made the first deep playoff run in the school's history. After winning our first three games of the sectional playoffs, we found ourselves in the semi-finals, pitted against the regional powerhouse Los Gatos. Los Gatos had garnered its fame not only from its success, but also because of the man who had helped bring it to them—their miraculous head coach, Charlie Wedemeyer.

Charlie had contracted A.L.S. (Lou Gehrig's disease), but had continued to coach in spite of it for years. By the time we met, Charlie's disease had progressed to the point that he was on the sideline in a golf cart with a ventilator. Because he was incapable of speech or hand signals, with his wife in headphones of her own, he would call plays, with a series of blinks that she would translate into signals for the quarterback and words for the coaches. His life, and that season in particular, became the basis for a made-for-TV movie, with our contest as a centerpiece.

The game was a grueling back-and-forth affair, with turnovers and touchdowns leading to a tie at 14 going into the final play. Charlie then sent his field goal unit onto the field, and they won on the strength of that kick 17-14. It was the only time in my life that I've had the press knocking me over to speak with an opposing coach who out-handicapped me. It was also one of the few times that I've felt a loss was as much sweet as it was bitter. Charlie's story was a phenomenal one, and he capped it with a title the next week. Even after the sting of our loss, I was capable of appreciating it. Even more than his victory was the way he had done it, with his wife by his side, each paying attention to the most minute of the other's movements. He was the living embodiment of the importance of the little things. Even though my team had given his squad everything that they could handle, I held him up as a model of what a man and his wife could accomplish. That was also what made the loss so bitter. Melanie's and my divorce would be finalized shortly after that season.

Chapter 15 | I Already Knew Life Wasn't Perfect, but Thanks for the Reminder

I don't know if paying close attention to the details of a football program prevented me from paying attention to the details of my marriage to Melanie. On the other hand, after moving to Gilroy, something in our relationship changed. We decided that rather than looking for a job, Melanie would stay home with Tim. It seemed right. After all, that was what both of our mothers had done. It wasn't, however, something that we could really afford if we ever wanted to be able to buy a house in Gilroy. In order to belay the loss of her income, I needed to do something extra. I'd coached two sports and advised the band in Livingston. In reality, however, I couldn't let it interfere with the football program I'd committed to building in Gilroy.

We decided that I'd make my extra money in the classroom, either by taking classes so I could move up the pay scale or by teaching summer school. Financially, this strategy worked out. In our second year in Gilroy, we were able to buy a house. That purchase, however, only put more of a burden on us. We had bought a fixer-upper. We didn't have the money to pay someone to fix it, and I didn't have the time to do it myself. I managed to give Tim every spare moment I had, but that didn't leave much time for Melanie. Between being cooped up with Tim and stuck in a community where she knew virtually no one, I would imagine Melanie was mind-numbingly bored. So, when we did have our fleeting moments to converse, they were usually about problems with the house or disagreements about how we were going to raise Tim. It was a recipe for discontent. As a result, by our third year in Gilroy, we both knew where we were headed.

Still, when I saw the finalized divorce papers, I was devastated. I knew that we each had needs that hadn't been met. Those were the types of things, however, that you worked through. While I knew we weren't rich, we were certainly better off than either of our families had been when we were growing up. I also knew that things were better between us than they were for my parents when they divorced. We'd probably gotten married too fast, but that just meant we were destined for growing pains. What we needed was counseling, not a dissolution of our marriage.

Thankfully, Melanie agreed to see a counselor with me, but she insisted that we separate. So, during my most triumphant season to date as a coach, I was living in a run-down apartment, fighting for every moment that I could find to see my son. At the same time, I was pouring out my heart and soul, so that a licensed marriage counselor could examine them and excoriate me.

By the time we had lost in the semi-finals to a coach who managed not only a disability but a marriage, I was certain my life was over. While coaches and players immediately began talking about the next season, I began thinking about my next job.

Gilroy was a great town—supportive, excited, and small. Small enough to be excited about a garlic festival and small enough that no matter how much I tried to avoid it, I would run into Melanie. Each time was like salt on the wound, because Tim would be with her. Furthermore, at the end of each conversation, no matter how well it went, he would go home with her. And, she wasn't moving. If I was going to achieve any sort of sanity, it would have to be me to leave.

But where was I going to go?

As with many of the moves that I've made in my life, the opportunity came just when I needed it. The coach who had preceded me at Livingston, Larry Nigro, had become an assistant coach at Merced High School. He called to ask if I was interested in coming to the biggest school in the valley. I told him I'd think about it, but that I'd have to get back to him. In reality, I had quite a bit going on at the moment. Larry let me ponder the situation for a couple days, before calling back to see if I'd made the decision.

I informed him that it was a difficult decision, which involved leaving a good school, with good facilities, and a sophomore quarterback in Jeff Garcia who could be something special (Jeff went on to win the Grey Cup in the Canadian Football League before becoming a Pro Bowl quarterback in the NFL). Larry informed me that Merced was a talent-laden team that had underachieved for most of its existence. I let him know that I had always been intrigued by underachievers. On the other hand, I would still need some time to think.

Two days later, Larry called again, curious if I'd finally made up my mind. I told him I hadn't. Furthermore, in all honesty, I had just gotten divorced and leaving Gilroy for Merced would mean moving away from my son. He apologized. Subsequently, after discussing my depressing situation, he said not to worry because they'd be able to lure someone out to Merced, if for no other reason because it was about the only place left in California with reasonably priced houses.

After our conversation (and his flip comment), I decided to do some research on the actual price of houses in Merced. I discovered that the same house would cost half as much in Merced as it would in Gilroy. Without thinking about the consequences, I began to run the numbers on how much I was paying in rent in Gilroy and what that amount might be able to buy in Merced. I realized that I would be able to get a little two-bedroom place in Merced for what it cost for a one-bedroom apartment in Gilroy.

If I moved to a town 90 minutes away, I would be able to own my own home, have a room for my son, and not have to see my ex-wife every other day shopping for fresh produce. But, it was 90 minutes away—how often would Tim actually stay in his room?

I spent several nights thinking about that decision, reevaluating the previous night's decision, and praying about my newest decision. Finally I came to a definitive one. I was moving to Merced.

I didn't inform Gilroy of my decision until it was a done deal. Once I had found out, however, that I had gotten the job (after again being the second choice), Gilroy handled it about as well as could be expected. Coming off a run to the semi-finals, they were more than a little shocked by the resignation. When I informed them, however, that I had come to Gilroy with a set of expectations for both football and for my life and that my life had dramatically changed, they seemed willing to accept the inevitable. I was leaving Gilroy forever.

On the other hand, that didn't mean I was leaving immediately. I still had the spring semester to teach in Gilroy. This schedule presented a bit of a problem for a program the size of Merced. Spring practice was when a coach laid the foundation for the upcoming season. Rather than start practice two hours after students got out of school in order to allow for my rush-hour drive time, Merced paid for me to have a last-period release. In other words, during spring ball, I would teach six periods (with a working lunch), hustle out to my car, intent on making the drive in less than an hour and a half so that I could start practice on time, coach for two hours, and then make the same drive home. I was hopeful that I could get home before Tim's bedtime, so that I could call to see how his day went. Sometimes, I caught him, and sometimes I didn't.

By the weekend, I was exhausted. I would find myself sitting on my bed, looking back at the week and wondering what I'd really accomplished (other than deepening the ruts on the highway). I wasn't the teacher I could be. I wasn't the coach I could be. Even more importantly, I definitely wasn't the father I could be. Even when Tim was with me in Merced, I found myself thinking about the work that I needed to complete before the next week began.

The irony was readily apparent. I was a coach who constantly harped on his players to be in the moment, and I couldn't lay on the floor to wrestle with my son, without thinking about the round of essays that I had to grade or the practice plan that I had to develop. I needed to do something … and that something was to get primary custody of Tim.

After talking to everyone I could think of and calling several different firms, I hired the best attorney I could afford (which isn't saying much). I managed to get court date quickly. Subsequently, after several interviews with my lawyer, I felt confident that I could win my custodial case on the grounds that I was the better parent.

When the final gavel came down, one thing was apparent: I'd gotten drilled.

After avoiding eye contact with Melanie, and a perfunctory handshake with my attorney, I was able to hug Tim. I managed to fight back the tears for his sake, but my heart broke as I watched him leave the courtroom with his mother. Not only had I lost my son, I also had to pay for the unfolding scenario with money I didn't have. By the time I'd gotten to my car, I felt like I had a complete and total understanding of two things: why there is such a big market for anti-depressants and that it didn't matter to me if I had to pay monthly rent to Highway 132. I was going to make the trip from Merced to Gilroy as often as I could. I was going to be a good father.

Over the next year, rather than buy a house as had been my original plan, I maintained two apartments—one in Merced and one in Gilroy. When we had a road game, I would arrange our weekend coaches' meetings for early Saturday morning and late Sunday evening so that I could spend virtually the entire weekend with Tim in Gilroy. For home games, Melanie would drop Tim off at the stadium before kickoff. In my mind, this schedule meant a good hour before the whistle blew; for Melanie, it sometimes meant a good minute.

My coaches knew that the ambiguity of this situation kept me on edge, and they would use it to amuse themselves by giving me "false sightings," starting about 45 minutes until kickoff. The more they did it, the more fired up I'd get. Whenever Tim did finally get to the stadium, he was in charge of the game ball. In other words, if the ball wasn't being used on the field it was in his hands. It also meant that, should we *want* to use it on the field, he should have it ready to go. In reality, this assignment can be more difficult than it sounds for an eight-year-old.

I'll never forget, before a playoff game during my third year of coaching at Merced, the referee sidled up to me a minute before kickoff, wanting to inspect the game ball. I turned to where Tim usually stood on my right to get the ball from him. He wasn't there. I turned to my left—not there either. Quickly scanning the sideline, I realized that he was nowhere to be found. I hollered at the coaches who were in close proximity to me to see if they knew where he'd gone; they had no idea. I was beginning to get frantic—I'd already lost custody of my son; now I had lost him altogether.

I was about ready to run up to the public announcer's box to put out an all-call, when one of my players told me that he thought he'd seen Tim wandering over to the concession stand. I shot a quick glance to the referee, who gave me a look that said, "Look, the only thing I need from the concession stand is that game ball." I then took off running toward the far end zone. By the time I got there, Tim was at the front of the line, cradling the game ball in both arms as he gawked at the board behind the cashier. He was so enthralled with our impressive candy selection that he didn't even notice when I took the ball and jogged back to the field so the game could kickoff.

Regardless of Tim's attentiveness during the game, after it was over, he would join us in the locker room and hang out until it was time to go home for the weekend. In fact, it was during the football season that I felt like I was a good father. We had a routine, and Tim seemed to love every minute he spent on the field with me.

When the season was over, while we would still see each other every chance we got, at least for him, it wasn't as special. My first winter in Merced, I drove up in the middle of the week for his Christmas concert. The production involved the entire school. As a result, Tim and his class only had two songs that they sung. When it was over, Melanie and I had worked it out that I would get to take Tim out for ice cream. Three words into my conversation with Tim, I discovered he'd already made other plans—he wanted to go out with his friends instead. Facing a second 90-minute drive, one in which a crappy Christmas concert served as the lone intermission, I realized that, despite my best efforts, Tim and I were destined to have the same relationship I'd had with my father—only through sports.

Or, so I thought.

Chapter 16 There's a First Time for Everything

If I was somehow able to remove the emotions of my personal life from the equation (in reality, every individual—if anyone—who has managed to achieve that in any measure certainly has life figured out more than I do), I would have to say that the move to Merced was an uncomfortable success. That interesting dichotomy began in the first meeting I held with the coaches. It was the spring, before I'd even taught a class in Merced, and we were in one of the other coach's rooms. I walked to the front and plainly laid out my expectations for the next year, explaining how much time they could expect to spend watching film, in meetings, and on the field.

In response, there seemed to be polarized, visceral reactions. About half of the staff were nodding and wondering if the meetings and film sessions could begin tonight. In contrast, the other half formed a line in front of me that turned into a "thanks, but no thanks" procession. The realization that this season was going to be more than a little different extended from the coaches to the players. Even I wasn't immune to the change.

As we moved into spring practice, and I watched some of our guys labor through the lightest of workouts, I called over Jerry McClanahan, one of the assistants who'd decided to stick around. Jerry was the most in-shape 55-year-old that I'd ever met. In all honesty, I was certain that he could out-perform a good quarter of the team on any number of physical tasks.

"Hey Mac?"

Jerry jogged over from where our team was warming up. He must have noticed that I wasn't watching the team, because his "Yeah coach?" came out with trepidation.

I nodded across the school's athletic facilities and toward the baseball field. "How long do you think that it would take for you to run around that backstop, do 10 pull-ups, run back around that backstop, do 10 burpees, go back to the backstop, do 10 push-ups, and take one more lap around the backstop?"

"I don't know coach; can I let you know after practice?"

"No rush."

"Yeah, there is coach."

I looked at Jerry. "Why's that?"

Jerry locked eyes with me. "Because I want to coach a championship team before I retire."

I smiled. "That's the goal."

"Then, I'll let you know after practice."

It turned out that the circuit took Jerry between 12 and 15 minutes to complete the circuit, which worked perfectly, given that the limits for a football team were comprised of two types of players. On the last day of spring practice, I informed the team of what Coach Mac had done. Furthermore, I explained that how at the opening of fall camp, if you were a back, you would be expected to complete this conditioning test in less than 12 minutes, and if you were a lineman, it had to be done in 15 minutes or less. While there were a few groans, there were more comments about how if some old guy could do it in 12 minutes, they could do it in five. The same thought was going through my head, because I knew that if the players were even reasonably dedicated to our summer workout program, I figured that they would have no problem with the circuit. Even so, I had no intention of making that test the be-all/end-all for admission to fall camp. In fact, it was my intent to chalk up any failures to "a bad day." I just didn't know how deep-seeded the lack of commitment was for some of the players.

By the time summer rolled around, I was scrambling to coordinate the workout program for the players, teach the coaches their new schemes and techniques, and see Tim as often as possible. This schedule resulted in things falling through the cracks, on occasion. To my personal misfortune, they always seemed to pertain to my own well-being.

Finally, one afternoon, I'd managed to carve out a few minutes to pick up a washing machine for my new place. Of course, because those few minutes backed up to something more pressing, in this instance, the start of a weight-lifting session, I was in a hurry. As I was waiting for the Sears® clerk to wheel out my new Kenmore® three-speed, I became enamored of four fishing poles that were positioned across the showroom floor. It was as if I was living in a Norman Rockwell moment: four boys escaping from the usually watchful eye of a mother, who is busy eyeing four male mannequins dressed in outfits perfect for church that Sunday. When the poles' purveyors broke into the open, I half expected to encounter four freckle-faced bean-pole boys, with identical features, but increasing size. Instead, I watched as four of my largest linemen left the store, in no hurry to go anywhere, including weight-training.

It was then that I knew that it was going to take more than the threat of a conditioning test to change the culture of Merced. There was going to be no chalking missed times up to bad days. For the first (and only) time in my career, I was going to have to cut players.

On the first day of fall camp, following the conditioning test, I stood at the door of the classroom, where we were going to be outlining what the players could expect for both fall camp and the 1986 season. The players were asked to form a single file line. Subsequently, as they reached me, I gave them one of two directions: "go ahead" or "wait outside." In total, 12 guys were asked to wait outside. They were mostly seniors, a group that included the four fishermen, two of whom had started the year before. The 12 all knew that they had failed the conditioning test. Furthermore, the sheepish looks on their faces suggested that they thought they were going to get reprimanded before being let in the classroom. In reality, it came as a shock to them when they discovered their fate was quite different.

"Guys, research states it takes six weeks to get into great shape," I explained. "In failing the test, you showed me that you aren't anywhere close to great shape. In other words, it will take you all of camp and half the season to get to the point where you would be able to help this team. I am sorry to say that is too long for me or your teammates to wait for you. So, this year, none of you will be on the team."

Even before I saw the looks on those guys' faces, I felt bad for them. I couldn't imagine missing my senior year of football. Keep in mind, however, my actions were for the good of the program. That suspicion was confirmed when I walked into the classroom with the guys who had made the team. They looked at me with the kind of respect that I had never gotten from a team in a first meeting, before or since. They were ready to embrace the change, and I was ready to embrace it with them.

◆ ◆ ◆

That first season we went 7-4, with a first round exit in the playoffs. I was amazed … and disappointed. I had never coached a more physically talented team—virtually no one played on both sides of the ball. Our tailback went on to earn a scholarship to play division 1 football—and to have a team like that lose to every other playoff team in our league in preparation for a loss in a road playoff game was astounding. The staff, students, and community were equally amazed … and excited. That playoff appearance was the first in years for the moribund program, and to say that everyone was ecstatic would only be a slight overstatement. I was the only one questioning our performance.

Still, even I was buoyed by the excitement surrounding our team. I knew it was time to capitalize on this positive momentum. The last thing I (or anybody else) wanted was to have that season be a mirage—the statistical outlier of an inept program. I recognized that the turnaround I was attempting to orchestrate was going to be a multi-season endeavor. As such, the first year, I'd let the players know that there were going to be expectations about their commitment to the team. The second year, I was going to work on building the desire to commit to the team, their teammates, and themselves.

❖ ❖ ❖

Getting the players to be fired up about the *idea* of an off-season training regimen wasn't that difficult. All they could talk about was how the next step was to take down the big three: Davis, Downey, and Atwater. All I had to do was tell them that this would help get them to where they all wanted to go. But, for players to actually be fired up as they *performed* an off-season training regimen (i.e., pushing through their third set of squats on a third consecutive 100-degree day) would be something altogether different. While it is easy to get excited about the prospect of change, there is often pain in the execution, which is why I put the first painful task on the coaches.

After that first season was over, and I fell into the role of a "regular" teacher, I recognized that the battles on the football field weren't the only ones the players were fighting on behalf of the school. There was a stigma associated with attending Merced: The stigma of low-reading scores, high drop-out rates, and the fact that only 20 percent of graduates were being admitted to the California university system. As difficult as it was going to be to defeat the big three, all that was going to come down to was playing well and catching a few breaks on three different Friday nights. In contrast, not becoming one of the saddening statistics was a battle that had to be fought on a daily basis.

It was with that thought in my head that I summoned all of my coaches together and told them of my grand off-season plans.

"Are we going to clinics?"

"No."

"Conferences?"

"No."

"School visits?"

"No."

"Then, what are we doing?"

"We're going to get a picture from the college or junior/community college of every player who played here and then went on to play at the next level."

"Oh."

"Furthermore, I'd make the calls from the school—a lot of them are going to be long distance, and who knows how long we're going to be put on hold."

❖ ❖ ❖

The project that I thought was going to take only a couple of weeks took a couple of months. When it was completed, we had a floor-to-ceiling collage of players from every level—junior colleges, community colleges, small colleges, big colleges, and three from the NFL—for our players to look at each time I or anybody else was talking to them in the weight room. It was my goal to make those kids' hopes for bigger and better things tangible. If I could, then, their workouts weren't just about beating somebody in a different color jersey. Rather, they were about beating the odds.

Even with an inspirational montage of Merced alumni looming over them from the power-lifting platforms, the idea of our dingy pinkish-cream colored weight room serving as the portal to a better tomorrow seemed anti-climatic. As a result, on a weekend when Tim wasn't with me, I went out and bought several gallons of white, black, and orange paint. I also contacted a few of the coaches and players, and collectively, we made that place feel like it was an extension of the program. That evening, when it was finished, and everybody had left, I remember standing there, with my hand on the light switch, and taking one last moment to admire our work. Going forward, after the collage was placed back on the wall again, it would feel like players were entering a hallowed hall wherein they were being watched by former Merced luminaries. It was the kind of change that one couldn't help but love, even if I had done it without asking a single person's permission.

"Looks a little different than when I left on Friday."

I turned around at the sound of a familiar voice. The principal was standing behind me.

"How much did that cost you?"

"I, uh, well, spent a hundred dollars on the paint."

"I'll have a check for you tomorrow."

The attendance to summer sessions in our updated weight room doubled from the previous year, a change all but ensuring that we weren't going to have any problems with conditioning the next year. With more players came more problems. This time, they were of a sort that I hadn't anticipated. The biggest problem was of the kind that could divide the team into factions, factions with irrevocable differences. On the other hand, how was I to know that three quarters of my team wouldn't like my music?

As one of the most diverse schools in the state, our population ran not only the gamut socio-economically, but was made up of significant proportions of African-Americans, Hispanic-Americans, Hmong-Americans (one of the largest concentrations in the nation), and Caucasian-Americans. On the football team, the musical preference seemed to fall along those lines. As a result, in an act of perceived diplomacy, I declared that each day of the week would belong to a different ethnic group, with the last day belonging to the coaches. Among the players, my politically correct declarations came to be known by more colorful names (e.g., "black guy day;" "white guy day"). To my delight, but it was obvious they were buying in to music-related mandate. My only two rules were that the music had to be free of swear words and that no one could complain about the music. Sometimes, I would push the limits of the players' abilities to hold their tongues by playing opera the whole session, but it was amazing to see the players catching each other learning the words to songs that they might not have ever heard otherwise. In fact, in some cases, they were exposed to languages they might not have ever heard otherwise.

I could very easily say that the transformation of the culture surrounding our weight room was the crowning achievement of my second year at Merced. On a grander scale, however, that was the year that the program really became the one I had envisioned. That was the year I brought Vern Kellerman over from Gilroy to take over the defense and that was the year I really began to focus on what it truly meant to build a program. I began to read every book I could about team-building. I paid my way to every coaching clinic within driving distance. Furthermore, I made visits to every school I could whose football program I admired. As I headed into that second season, I was able to say unequivocally that Merced was my team. We went 4-6.

The excitement that had come from the community was gone. There was grumbling in the halls from the staff and students that it was the same old team. There were no playoffs for that group of outgoing seniors. But, there was no drama.

I didn't have to cut anyone. Everyone came to camp in shape. The parents didn't complain about the losses, and the kids didn't complain about playing time. In fact, everyone seemed as satisfied as they could be for a middle-of-the-pack team. Even the coaches weren't second guessing the calls made in the close games. It was as if everyone was satisfied with mediocrity. As competitive as I am, on occasion, I felt like I was the only one frustrated with the season. For that group of guys, however, it was the most wins they'd had at the school. For the juniors, they had quadrupled their win total of their freshman and sophomore seasons … combined. For them, 4-6 felt like the season of a lifetime. For me, it was a lesson in perspective. For all of us, it served as a stepping stone for the year to come.

Chapter 17 The Snowball Effect

As I've gotten older, I've discovered that it isn't until your third year of doing something or being somewhere that you get comfortable. Up to that point in my life, outside of high school, I hadn't really been anywhere for more than two years. Menlo, Azusa, Menlo, North Monterey, Livingston, Gilroy—I don't know if it was youthful indiscretion, ambition, opportunity, or a rare ability to wear out my welcome, but change always seemed to come to me every two years. So, when that third year rolled around at Merced, I must have subconsciously known that I wasn't going to change my own life. Something was going to have change my life for me in order to keep the streak alive. I just didn't expect it to come in the package that it did.

Before the season (and school year) even began, I received word that Melanie was going to be moving with Tim to a mountain resort in Southern California. I knew this meant that seeing him was going to be more difficult than ever. Personally, I had faith that not only would I continue to be the best father I could, but that things would turn out the way they were supposed to. Still, the notion that my son was no longer a short highway trip away left an emotional void that had to be filled. Strangely enough, it was the school that provided the filler.

Toward the end of my second year of teaching at Merced, we were presented with a sobering statistic about our student body: between 40 and 50 percent would drop out. As that number washed over us, the administration's explanation of the programs they were investigating to address the issue were drowned out by my own thoughts. In my mind, football had been critical in not only keeping kids in school, but in giving them the motivation to pass classes. I had watched teammates tutor each other to ensure they were eligible for the next week's game. In addition, I had held team-study sessions to help students not only improve their GPA, but also their prospects for college. Furthermore, I had spoken to the coaches of other programs, and from what I could gather, they were doing the same sort of things. In a transcendent moment, it also occurred to me that in a school of over 3,000 students, who was providing that kind of support for the non-athletes? Who was ensuring that they were passing their classes?

By the time my ruminations had ended, the meeting was over, and I was being approached by the principal. He asked if I'd be interested in the new drop-out program. My first instinct was to tell him that a name change might be in order. On the other hand, upon realizing that I hadn't heard most of its explanation, I couldn't offer much in the way of a different one. Instead, I told him that I was interested.

That summer, I found out that my interest had gotten me enrolled in a two-week interactive listening class. The class was going to provide me with a crash course in team-teaching a daily group counseling session for which students would get social studies credit. Because every school in the district was going to be implementing this program, each had sent both the teacher and the counselor who were going to be guiding the group's interactions. The counselor working with me was my future wife, Sue, who had been at Merced the same length of time as me, but whom I had never met before the training session.

From the first "weather report," we ran around the circle—students might say they were "sunny" when things were good; "cloudy with a chance of rain" when things weren't great or uncertain; or "a tornado just blew through" if all hell had broken loose at home—I knew that Sue and I were a good match. Sue was a well-respected professional counselor, who was well-versed in helping students navigate their feelings. In contrast, I was her irreverent comedic sidekick, ready to make fun of myself at a moment's notice.

Each day, we had an agenda where we would bring up a concept like "personal values" and go around the circle, giving each person an opportunity to speak. We'd made a promise to the students on the first day that we would never push them to talk outside of giving a daily weather report. As a result, in the beginning of our sessions, on a number of occasions, the only people who would share would be Sue and me. It was an amazing way to get to know someone—being forced to bare your soul and expose your flaws in front of 15 teenagers, who were considered drop-out risks, as well as an adult, who had once only known your name from an employment roster. It was also a lot less expensive than dinner and drinks. I came to find that not only did Sue laugh at my stories, but that I could laugh at hers, and that both of us were living with the pain of a previous divorce and struggling to find our way through the minefield of split-parenting.

With this unique combination of humor and sorrow, trials and triumphs didn't just serve to open Sue and I up to each other. It also helped to open the students up to the group. The students became comfortable with explaining that "it was f*&#ing hailing last night," meant that a student had been up all night at the hospital with her mom after she'd been decked by her dad. Through stories like that, students began to connect to each other through experiences that had been shared on opposite ends of town and in the context of very different cultures.

That students were getting social studies class credit for these sessions may have been considered fishy by some of the traditionalists in the district, but the students were right where they needed to be on Maslow's hierarchy. On the other hand, you can't worry about how the world works until you feel that your world is safe and that you are valued within it. I remember thinking that some of those students deserved a standing ovation for just being at school. Frankly, the thought that this class may have provided some of the impetus behind their attendance inspired me. I'd always felt like I was changing lives on the field. Now, I was also changing lives in the classroom. It was as if I was on the cusp of something special.

I don't know if the football players could feel my inspiration or had found some of their own, but that group of woebegone seniors decided this was going to be the year that *they* did something special. We started off the season by winning our modest schedule of non-league games, beating a series of teams we should have and providing us with a bit of momentum, as we headed into the gauntlet that was our league.

Once we were into the heart of the season, it felt like that momentum began to snowball. We started beating the weaker teams in our league by three touchdowns, and we eked out wins against the big three points. Before I knew it, we were the undefeated league champions. In reality, I had no idea why. At every single position, I could point to another team in the league and say they had a more talented guy. Going into a number of the contests, I could look across the sidelines and see a more talented team. It just seemed like every break went our way.

Personally, I thought that we were simply the luckiest team in the league. In retrospect, I have come to appreciate the prescience of John F. Kennedy's statement that "luck is when preparation meets opportunity" (my family, after all, was raised in emulation of the Kennedys). This precept has continually manifested itself on the football field, beginning for me, with that team. That group of guys had been preparing for that moment for the past three years. When their moment had finally come, luck was finally on their side.

Their momentum continued, without pause, until the section championship, a game we ultimately lost 35-21, after having the lead well into the third quarter. No school from our conference had ever won a section championship, and few had ever even made it. It appeared that there were lots of leagues much better than ours. In my mind, I was certain that that game was going to be my one and only shot.

But, the momentum kept growing. Players were in the weight room the day after the season ended, wanting to get started on next season's training. Assistants were in my classroom the next week, raiding my cupboards for game film to develop the scheme that would push us over the top. Coaches from other teams were coming by the next month to pick my brain. In addition, people from all over the valley were beginning to ask if I had ever thought of publicly speaking about how I'd gone from being born with no hands to successfully running a football program at out-of-the-way Merced High School.

The momentum that had begun in the classroom for me swept its way onto the football field, came back to the classroom, and carried away my personal life as well. I had asked Sue to marry me. We hadn't been dating that long, but it shouldn't have been a surprise, considering that our first date ended at a Chinese restaurant, with a fortune cookie that read "You will be married within a year." Besides, because of our classroom, we were spending more time together than any dating couple I've ever met. When our students found out that we were getting married that coming summer, they were very excited. As such, the next few classes turned into de facto wedding showers. In fact, the only hitch in our entire courtship was at the wedding ceremony itself.

Sue and I had found a wonderful little church, had invited a select group of friends and family (as well as a couple of students), and had written our own vows. We'd also found roles for each of the three kids: Lisa and Julie were going to be flower girls, and Tim would be the ring/chain bearer. Sue and I had decided that, since it is the circular nature of the ring that is its most important quality, my "ring" would go around my neck in the form of a gold chain. It was as sound a game plan as I'd ever devised. But as with anything else, you can't plan for every contingency. Accordingly, when it came time for the pastor to ask Sue to place the "ring" on my person, neither of us had anticipated his phrasing: "Sue, you may now place the chain around Mark's neck."

I couldn't help but laugh, neither could Sue, nor anybody else in the audience. I haven't laughed that hard very many times in my life, and I still find myself smiling about it, from time to time, because the chain is still there, around my neck.

The whole story—from co-teaching a class for drop-out risks to having our fortune cookie come true to the bungled climax of our wedding ceremony—was the kind of thing one would think could only exist in a Hollywood confection of a non-traditional classroom. Subsequently, as Sue and I discussed with the students where we had gone for our honeymoon, we discovered something else that could have been a movie-studio invention: most of our students had never seen the ocean, even though it was only two hours away. We decided right then that if those students could help us discover each other, the least we could do was help them discover something that they'd never seen. We were going to take them to see the Pacific Ocean.

As we organized the trip, we decided that we would enrich the experience by going to the beach by way of Carmel and show the students the mansions in the hills looking down at the water. When we got there, I felt a little bit like Robin Leach. On the other hand, since we hadn't been granted access to any of the homes and the fact that "Lifestyles of the Rich and Famous" wasn't one of the kids' favorite shows, I didn't attempt to get into character too much. The notion that people owned these houses, but didn't even live in them (most were "summer" homes of very wealthy people) kept the students talking all the way down to the beach.

After a picnic lunch on the sand and a stroll along the water (for Sue and I, it was a stroll—for the students, it was more of a splash-and-dash), we finished the trip at an outlet mall, where I learned that you really can't have enough ways to say, "Now, put that back." On the way back to Merced, the students, who six months before had been reticent to give a personal weather report, talked non-stop about what they'd seen, felt, and almost bought, creating conversational threads that would carry through the next week of school. It was a rousing success. Even more importantly, without giving it too much thought, Sue and I knew it was something that we needed to do with every group of students.

The next year, the students thought they could do better than the last. They wanted to go on a roller coaster. Sue thought the sort at the local county fair would do the trick, but I knew what the kids were thinking—Magic Mountain. Sue and I both knew it would be expensive. As an outgrowth of running a football program that survived solely on fundraising, I called a couple of my vendors. To enrich the experience, we had the students run some numbers, and they determined that if every one of them sold two boxes of candy, we'd have enough to go on the trip.

When the chocolate bars had been sold, the permission slips filled out, and the vans lined up, I went to the principal, excited to share our plan.

"You're going to Magic Mountain?"

"Yeah, we already raised all the money."

"But, the trip has to be educational."

"It is. We determined how much money we'd need, we learned some sales skills, and we budgeted for every aspect based on our net profit."

"No. You're still going down there to ride roller coasters. That's not educational."

"But—"

"Sorry. The answer is no."

When I brought the news back to the students, I may have been frustrated, but they were devastated. Sue didn't have time to react personally. She must have been wondering how much counseling she was going to have to do after these disadvantaged students were faced with yet another setback. This situation was going to make the end of the year as awkward as the beginning. Only, in this instance, we'd already blown all of our good ice-breaking stories. Then a thought struck me—what if we went down there under the guise that it was a college visitation? After all, there was a college right next to the park—the California Institute of Art. Part of the impetus behind the development of this class had been that less than 20 percent of our students were eligible for the California university system. How could the principal say no to us investigating our students' options after they graduated?

I ran this "new" idea by the principal. In response, he gave us the go ahead, just so long as we did as we said we were going to do—visit the college. Because Sue was uncomfortable misleading the California Institute of Art, it became her job to buy the tickets to Magic Mountain, and my role was to organize the trip to the California Institute of Art. I was able to book their earliest tour at 10:00 a.m., which meant that between a three-and-a-half-hour drive and at least one rest-stop break, we needed to leave Merced before 6:00 a.m.

With such an early departure, I thought it would be safe to assume that the drive down would involve Sue, me, coffee, and two vans full of sleeping students. Those kids, however, showed up on fire. Furthermore, by the time we got to the college, they were so excited that I was, quite frankly, afraid for the Art Institute's tour guide. That fear grew when the guide informed us that they only provided tours to seniors in high school.

I pursed my lips, avoided eye contact with Sue, and looked at our students. "That won't be a problem, we're all seniors here." As I spoke, I nodded dramatically, eyeing the freshmen and sophomores in the group to make sure that they understood what I was saying.

"Well, great. Let's start the tour."

When we entered our first building, the students came upon their first piece of art—they found themselves standing on the image of a 20-foot-long erect penis. As Sue and I tried to stifle the twitters, as the kids realized what they were walking across, our hushed voices were drowned out by the sound of bongos. Upon our exit from the building, we discovered the source of the percussive rhythms—a dread-locked gentleman dressed in what looked like a tye-dyed mumu. The students scrutinized every inch of the guy, but he seemed immune to their gazes. He was lost in the music.

By the time our kids had recovered, the tour guide was explaining how several of the college's students were already doing work for Disney's animation department. This information was something with which our students could associate. As a result, they began to ask questions, questions about which movies, about how the students were able to get jobs with Disney, and about the kind of courses that you had to take to get to draw cartoons for a living. The tour guide seemed inspired by their interest and attempted to answer every one of their questions in excruciating detail. While Sue and I were beginning to get bored, our students were eating it up. That connection led the guide to tell us that they were going to be performing a play after lunch if we wanted to stick around, and that he could probably get us passes to the commons so that we could eat and chat with the students.

Before anyone could tell him that we were leaving for Magic Mountain (or worse, ask what the play was), I informed the guide that we were on a tight schedule, what with our pre-med students needing to visit UCLA after this and all.

By the time we thanked the guide, navigated around the building with the phallic floor, and got back to the vans, it was 11:00, the normal opening time for Magic Mountain. We were to the park in less than 15 minutes and got a great parking spot—one of the five best in the place. My first thought was that the kids were going to be so exhausted with participating on roller coasters in two hours that we'd be back in time for dinner. My second, more troubling, thought came after I noticed none of the rides were moving. In fact, the park was closed. I got my confirmation from the chain wrapped around the gates and the shuttered window at the ticket booth.

I turned to my wife. "Sue, you reserved the tickets."

"I know. I…"

The feeling of déjà vu swept over me, and though I knew *I* had never been through this before, I experienced the kind of kindred celluloid spirit that Clark Griswold had shared with the world. Granted, I hadn't driven all this way with a dead body on the roof of the vehicle. On the other hand, Chevy Chase's character from *National Lampoon's Vacation* didn't have a van full of troubled teenagers. Clark's solution had been simple: forcibly enter the park and hold the security guard hostage, while his family caught all of the rides they wanted.

Sue and I were attempting to teach our students the importance of rational decision-making. Somehow, a felony breaking-and-entering charge seemed outside of that particular scope of thought. Still, these were kids who hadn't had a lot of victories in their lives and for them to suffer another defeat on our watch would not only devastate them, but also the credibility of our program. The possibility of going back to the play at the Art Institute flashed through my mind, but when I heard a tragic sob in the background, I knew we needed another solution.

"How come we're not going in?"

"Is the park closed?"

"Are you kidding me? I got up at five in the morning for this? This is f—"

I cleared my throat to prevent profanity from taking over the students' mouths. "We're going to Disneyland." Sue gave a nervous laugh. "That's not what the permission slip says." "I went to school down here and it's only 30 miles away. We should be there in a half hour, 45 minutes tops." There was some grumbling from the students, but for the most part, they took it pretty well.

Sue still seemed to be on the fence. "Mark, we barely got permission to come here, and even then it was under false pretenses. I completely understand what you're trying to do, and I'm going to support whatever you choose to do, but I just want to make sure you see the other side of this. We are now going somewhere else, somewhere even farther away, somewhere we don't have tickets for, somewhere—"

"Sue, we said we'd get them on roller coasters, and we're going to get them on roller coasters." Sue looked at me and I knew that she knew I wasn't going to budge on this. "Okay, let's do this."

About an hour into our two-and-a-half-hour trip through LA traffic I was made perfectly aware of my decision by the tempers that were flaring behind me. The kids nerves were fried, Sue's nerves were fried. My nerves were fried. The only thing keeping me going was the notion that we had driven all this way to get our kids on some rides, and by God, we were going to get our kids on some rides (I guess I was even more like Clark Griswold than I thought).

By the time we got to Disneyland, it was 2:00 in the afternoon. Thankfully, the park was open. Sue and I rustled all of the students out of the van, herded them toward the entrance, and set our cash box in front of the clerk. We'd budgeted the trip down to the exact penny and triple-checked before we'd left that we'd have enough for each and every ticket—at Magic Mountain. Admission to Disneyland was nearly double that amount, so after Sue and I had used our credit cards to get the students in, we informed them that they would have six hours in the park. We were going to be meeting by the entrance at eight o'clock to gather for the return trip home.

I can't tell you what the kids did for that six hours. Frankly, I think Sue and I only saw them once, while we were in the park. More fortuitously, however, we had all them accounted for and back in the vans by 8:45 p.m. Although such a timeline was not great, by that time Sue and I were both exhausted. As a result, we didn't have the energy to do much more than raise an eyebrow. The cacophony of the student's talking over each other with their stories from the park kept us all awake for the first hour of the drive back. By 10 o'clock, however, only Sue and I were left awake. So, after we'd dropped our last student off at his house, taken the school's van back, and driven home in our own car, we discovered that we'd put in a 24-hour day—5 a.m. to 5 a.m. Among a lot of memorable trips with kids in that program (and we had one every year), that was one we will never forget. I'm also pretty sure that none of those kids will forget it either.

While you can plan on having a culminating event in a classroom, planning a culminating event for a football team is much more difficult. For one thing, you never know when your season is going to end. Our players decided, however, that they were going to try and make it easy for me. They chose to go on an eight-year run of league titles. The section title game we'd lost ended up providing those juniors with all of the experience that they needed to play for the championship again. Only this time, they won.

The game itself must have been fun to watch, as is any game when it gives the coach heart palpitations on the sideline. In reality, Disneyland paled in comparison to the emotional roller coaster of being a part of that contest. The game was played at the old UC Davis field, and the place was packed—13,000 people standing shoulder-to-shoulder to watch two 13-0 teams battle for the section title. The stadium was pretty evenly divided in its support for the two schools.

For the first part of the game, most of the eruptions came from our side, as we went up 14-0. Our opponent, Nevada Union, came storming back, taking the lead. After several lead changes after the half, we found ourselves down 29-28 with, well, not a lot of time left to play. Normally, I'd know exactly how much time, but because the scoreboard clock had gone out, the referees were giving us updates on the amount of time left in the game. We managed to drive down into field goal range. I then called a time-out—not because we needed to stop the clock, but because Nevada Union had an amazing field goal block unit. The week before, we'd installed a new formation to combat it. As such, I wanted to make sure everyone was comfortable with it. After they assured me that that they were, I jogged back off the field, half-expecting Nevada Union to take a time-out to ice our kicker.

Instead, I did.

It was obvious from the sideline that confusion still existed among the players. Rather than go back out there myself, I sent out our offensive line coach—the guy who'd drawn up the scheme—to ensure everyone had it down, since the section championship was riding on that kick.

He must have done a better job explaining it than I did, because the players lined up correctly, blocked confidently, and watched as the smallest guy on our team put the ball through the uprights, winning us both our school's and our league's first section championship. The celebration afterwards was terrific. Players hugging players, players hugging coaches, and players hugging their parents. It wasn't until after that game that I learned how many of our players' dads had played for Merced. Subsequently, when they came up to thank me, they made me feel as if I'd given them the greatest gift they'd ever received—the title they'd never gotten for their sons. I couldn't imagine it getting better than that.

Then, we won it all again the next year. In the process, we finished #1 in the state.

With California being so large, it is logistically impossible to have playoffs for the entire state, which is why it's broken up into sections. So, while every California coach's goal at the beginning of each season for his team is to win the section championship, it is the dream of every coach in California to finish #1 in the state. To achieve such a title, a team not only has to impose its will on each and every one of its opponents, it also has to impress each and every one of the poll voters. Typically, schools with a track record for titles and undefeated seasons are those that start off high enough in the polls to have a chance. Our first title team, with only a loss in the previous year's section championship game to mar its record, didn't have a realistic chance at finishing first in the state. In contrast, our 1990 team, with two consecutive berths in the title game and one undefeated season to stand on, had a legitimate chance in the eyes of the voters. Not surprisingly, we entered the season ranked #2, behind only the powerhouse Morse High School of San Diego. It was a great place to be, and it was an honor to be ranked up there with one of the best programs in the state. In reality, however, I kind of figured that we wouldn't climb any higher than that. In terms of having a tradition of winning, we couldn't hold a candle to Morse.

With that mindset, we just plugged along through our pre-season schedule and the first part of our league schedule, winning each game pretty handily and remaining a solid second fiddle in the state rankings to Morse. The thing about that 1990 team was that we never lowered our level of play to that of our opponent. On the other hand, we managed to raise our game against the toughest competition whenever necessary. It was just a team with an intense focus. Or so I thought.

That focus manifested itself when we faced our most important test of the season against our rival Atwater. After the opening kickoff, we started to blow them out. It was an amazing thing to watch. Although I was happy about the way things were going, and

I could have easily started thinking about something else, I still was consumed by what was happening on the field. So, when a roar erupted from the crowd, and we were still in the huddle, I was confused. Subsequently, when our sideline erupted moments later after a two-yard run, I was even more perplexed. Finally, the word got to me. Someone in the stands had just learned that Morse had lost. As a result, we were going to be #1 in the state in the next week's poll.

I remember jokingly saying to one of the players that now all that we had to do was win the rest of our games the way we were winning this one. He (and the rest of the team) must have taken me seriously, because they did, finishing #1 in the state, as well as in the top 10 in the *USA Today* nationwide poll.

Seeing our name in a newspaper that was widely distributed across the United States, from Florida to Alaska, was the crowning achievement for that group of seniors. In reality, it could very easily be considered the greatest achievement of my coaching career. On the other hand, to state that it was even the best moment of that year for me would be a lie. Somehow, the positive momentum that had been snowballing for me, personally and professionally, had finally reached the part of my life it had consistently missed: Tim was going to be coming to live with me in Merced.

We were going to be a family again.

Chapter 18 Is It Getting Hot in Here? (I Don't Know, but That Snowball Sure Looks Like It's Melting)

When Sue and I got married, I started to feel like I was a part of a family again. Sue had two girls, Julie, who was two, and Lisa, who was nearly eight (a year older than Tim). Suddenly, I felt like a full-time parent again. Almost.

Before I became a step-dad, I had no idea about how difficult it was to walk that fine line between parenting and being a kid's parent. When it came to dropping the girls off at school, going to their games, or transmitting news through the house, I felt like I was handling my new gig with aplomb. On the other hand, when a need arose to discipline the girls (which wasn't that often), it didn't take much to elicit the "You're not my daddy!" response. While that statement is seemingly boilerplate for step-children, and there should be an equally standard response for parents, frankly, I never knew what to say to the girls after that. I have never felt more powerless in my life. Thank goodness, Tim came to visit once a month. His arrival entailed more than just a chance to hang out with my son; it was also an opportunity to boost my parenting ego.

The thing is, as tough as it was for me to find my place in the family, it was probably much more difficult for Sue and the girls to figure out how to adjust to living with me. Sue, as a single parent, had raised her girls in her image. They were respectful, well-behaved, and terrifically tidy. If their life was one of our classroom weather reports, it would have been mostly sunny, with a light breeze. At some point, Hurricane Mark blew into their lives. I disturbed everything. My papers covered every surface; my shoes were kicked off next to wherever I'd last sat down; and my dog had shed absolutely everywhere. Periodically, Tropical Storm Tim would swing through, doubling the damage. Yet, somehow those three girls weathered the storm. Finally, after two years, we reached a bit of an equilibrium. Then Tim came to *live* with us.

❖ ❖ ❖

While Tim was in Southern California, I had worked hard to compartmentalize my life. I focused on what I could control—football, my classroom, and my relationship with Sue and her kids. That one time a month that Tim would come up to visit, I would do everything I could to make it about him. After his two-night stay, however, I would put him back on the plane home. It would break my heart every time I watched him walk down the gangway, his little backpack bouncing with each step. I would find myself torn about whether I wanted him to turn back and wave as he took his turn toward the airplane. For me, an underlying question arose: was one last glimpse of his face worth the agony I'd feel as it disappeared? While the walk to the car afterwards was always miserable, by the time I had pulled into the driveway, I was ready to move back into my compartmentalized life.

When Tim hit the fifth grade, I knew that he'd had a couple of rough years at school. For example, at one parent-teacher conference I'd been in town for, his teacher informed me that Tim had begun bawling "I want my daddy" in class. He, Melanie, and I always worked through it, however. Each year seemed to end with him in good standing. Something about the beginning of that year must have felt different, however, for both he and Melanie, because I got a call from her, informing me that she thought that he should come live with Sue and me. I couldn't have been more ecstatic. Sue and I were going to be able to build *our* family.

The first thing that we did with Tim was to enroll him in a private school in town, in the hope that the structure and smaller classes would help get him out of his academic rut. This decision had an additional benefit—the school was less than a mile away from the high school and our practice field. After he learned the route to the high school (1/4 of a mile down the street that fronted his school, a right turn, and then another 3/4 of a mile put him in the middle of our practice), it became the routine for Tim to attend practice with me after he was done at school. In fact, I had down to the minute exactly what time I should see Tim rolling through the practice field gates (3:11). As Tim got more and more comfortable with the guys on the team, he would gravitate to those players who gave him the most attention, positive or negative. Some thought he was the funniest thing that they'd ever seen. In contrast, others thought that he was the most obnoxious. For better or worse, however, he was as much a Merced Bear as they were.

It was the same way around the house, except that went for every one of us. For better or worse, we were a family. Sue and I did as much as we could to make it feel that way. We all attended each other's events; we all ate meals together; and we vacationed together. In reality, any one of our family-together events could go extraordinarily well or extraordinarily bad.

We quickly figured out that there was no way anything we did was going to please all of the kids. As a rule, we could usually get two out of three. At that point, one goal became to make sure that we never displeased the same kid twice in a row. As a result, our family trips were wildly disorganized. On occasion, an "i" didn't get dotted, a "t" didn't get crossed, or a dog didn't get put in the garage after the dinner had been set on the table. The latter scenario often resulted in the family returning from a trip to the movie store to find every plate licked clean. Frankly, I was happy that both Sue and I were teachers, because modifying and adjusting became a way of life.

Although the efforts involved in building our family were at least reasonably successful, the situation came with a price: exhaustion. The whole time that we were pouring ourselves emotionally into each other's lives at home, Sue and I were pouring ourselves emotionally into our students' lives at school. Between those moments, Sue was grinding away at the sort of daily toils that keep a household functioning, and I was grinding away at the sort of daily toils that keep a football team functioning.

It wasn't possible for me to do everything everyone needed. In fact, there was many a night when Sue would come out to the living room to wake me in the chair where I'd fallen asleep watching film. Most nights, I'd follow her to bed to steal a couple of hours of sleep before we started it all over again. Some nights, I wouldn't. I'd go back to watching film. It was like my entire life was a sleep-deprivation study. Only, no one was telling me if I was passing or failing, though there were clear indications that could lead to reaching either conclusion.

Coincidentally, for Merced High School, it was the same way. With slightly over 50 percent of students graduating, and only 20 percent qualifying for the state university system, some individuals were quick to point out the school was a failure. In the eyes of others, with a football program on a run of historic proportions and a highly ranked school marching band, our school was a rousing success. Our lists of successes and failures were as diverse as the school's population, a notion that didn't escape a San Francisco TV station.

Before my sixth season at Merced, the state athletic commission was seeking to put together pre-season games between high profile programs. Being two-time section champions, we were slated to play De La Salle, runner-up in the San Francisco Bay Area section and one of the most renowned programs in the country. We were going to play at our place, with the national representative from De La Salle's district delivering the game ball by helicopter. Forget the section championships; this contest was going to be the biggest game our kids ever played.

Even though we had been named the #1 team in the state the year before, it was the first time that a spotlight had really been shined on our school. In reality, the natural juxtaposition between our giant public school and their small, exclusive private school was the kind of scenario over which the media drools. While there would be passing reference to the kind of obstacles our students had to overcome, most stories painted the match-up as Merced's wild bunch versus De La Salle's disciplined young men (i.e., the gangland Goliath versus the department store David).

Then, a local San Francisco TV news station put together a story about the kind of person you could find on the Merced football team. A one-minute vignette was devoted to me, the coach with no hands. Another was given to a typical Sunday in the life of one of our African-American students, following him from home, to church, and to an afternoon spent with his family. A third minute was about one of our Hmong players, while a fourth followed one of our Hispanic students. The last vignette followed one of our Caucasian players, as he went to school, played football, and worked on his family's farm. The station sent me a copy of the beautifully edited final piece. Even though we lost that game to De La Salle and their star receiver (an eventual New York Giant) Amani Toomer, I came out of the experience buoyed that the public perception of our school might just change.

The next week, I made copies and sent them to every member of the school board and our principal, with a note explaining that this information is the kind of thing that we should be excited to share with the public, as opposed to the fact that our students consistently finish in the bottom quartile in reading. Two years later, I heard back from one of the board member's wives on the matter. Her husband had found the tape when he was cleaning out the garage and thought that I should have it. It had never been opened. The note was either not read or ignored. It also crystallized for me the feelings that had been milling about in the back of my and every other coach and teacher's brain—we were overburdened and underappreciated.

I began to wonder why, if we were packing 9,000 people in the stands on Friday nights with tickets that were sold out on Tuesday, I had to sit in a fireworks stand on July 4, fund-raising rather than spending time with my family. I began to wonder why, if Sue and I were seeing tangible changes in the performance of our students, the district was talking about cutting our program. I began to wonder why, if I was teaching a full load, acting as department chair, and running a football program with 220 kids, I had to fight for the funds to take my coaches to clinics. Furthermore, I began to wonder why, if every other school in the league (many of which had similar socio-economic make-ups) could find money to upgrade their stadiums, we couldn't. I decided I needed to start making these thoughts known.

I went to the administration to ask if Sue's and my program was going to be around the next year. They replied that they'd have to get back to me. I went to the principal and asked about getting some of the concession revenue. He informed me that the money belonged to the school, not the program. I put together a slide-show and presentation on the need to improve our stadium facilities, in accordance with the rest of our section, and asked the board to levy a bond to pay for it. I was told that it would never work and was asked to not come to another meeting. Even for my players, the situation had started to get tired. On the bus after we had won in the semi-finals and were headed for a section championship, I overheard one kid ask another if he was going to get a ring to celebrate the appearance in the title game.

"No, I'll just get mine next year."

"Yeah, me neither."

At the end of my eighth season, my patience had begun to wear thin with the leadership of Merced. As a result, when a new high school—Golden Valley—was set to open the next year, I spoke to my principal in no uncertain terms.

"I know that the teachers with the most seniority are going to get first choice about staying here, but if you want to keep the football program strong, you should try to keep the coaches on staff."

"What do you mean?"

"Because coaches have less seniority than the rest of the teachers, if you keep only the most senior staff members, then you will lose most of the coaches to Golden Valley."

The principal scoffed. "I know that."

I was perplexed. "Then, why did you ask, 'What do you mean?'"

"I meant, this is Merced—our football team will always be good."

"Oh." I remembered what it had been like when I arrived. "I see."

Over the summer, most of my staff was transferred to Golden Valley. They had been forced into a new beginning.

I was going to choose mine.

Golden Valley looked to me like a golden opportunity.

Chapter 19 How Long Did It Take Sisyphus to Figure It Out?

Starting from scratch is never easy. You don't know what ingredients you already have, which ones you have to find, and which ones you could do without. It does, however, allow you to create just about anything you want. So, when I got to Golden Valley, I wasn't that worried about figuring out what we needed to do to put a playoff team on the field, because I knew that would come with time. What I wanted was to ensure that my players and coaches were not going to be engrossed in a legacy of demographic rifts or the gross under-achievement that I'd found at other schools. The Golden Valley program was going to be built on dedication—dedication to family, the school, the program, and to each other. In order to foster this spirit, I looked to the heart of any program, the weight room, for inspiration.

There was no inspiration to be found. There was no weight room.

In the process of the requisite (and bureaucratic) cost-cutting that goes into building a school, the designers had decided against adding a workout room for players—most likely, because of the prohibitive cost of equipment. They had, however, included a four-bay industrial arts/auto shop facility, forgetting the prohibitive cost of *that* equipment. I had found my muse.

After getting permission from the new principal to appropriate the auto shop for my weight room, the coaches and I began scouring the classifieds for used equipment. I found a couple of bankrupt gyms, looking to liquidate their assets. I also discovered some players and parents who knew how to weld that could build us squat racks. All told, my little truck's tired springs must have toted more than 50 loads of decrepit, rusty iron, creating the sort of hodgepodge facility that was usually reserved for the Hollywood underdogs. On the other hand, it was ours. Our team-building had already begun.

Even though the players and I had essentially built the weight room, it was hardly the kind of place on which you could hang your hat (we never knew when the hat hook—or anything else—might break). We needed something more, some sort of rallying cry. In looking at our team as they sweated through a summer workout, I realized that as a team without a senior class, it was going to be a challenge to keep every game close, much less win many of them. In staff meetings, our motto for the season became "make 'em keep their starters in the whole game." For a group of coaches who understood the value of experience, this plea was a legitimate rallying cry.

On the other hand, it wasn't the kind of thing that you could put on a team T-shirt. That required a slightly different tact.

As a movie buff with an appreciation for westerns, when I looked out at a team without its typical foundation for victory—seniors—it brought to mind a line from *The Treasure of the Sierra Madres*: "Badges? We don't need no stinkin' badges." With a couple of tweaks, I had come up with our team tag-line—"Seniors? We don't need no stinkin' seniors." I handed out the shirts the next week.

The players ate them up. It seemed like they couldn't wear them enough, and pretty soon, other students would stop by and ask if they could get a shirt. Even staff members would sidle up to me and ask if I had any extras. Everybody loved the shirts. Well, almost everybody.

In Merced, with summer temperatures always hovering near 100 degrees, you learn to always be on the lookout for heat stroke. I became keenly aware of the signs—nausea, dizziness, shortness of breath. The easiest symptom for me to identify, however, was a flushed face. So, I was surprised when one of the players showed up late for a workout short of breath … with an ashen face.

"What's up Jimmy? Are you feeling okay?"

"I—I'm fine coach."

"Are you sure? You look like you saw a ghost."

"Well, sir, I, um, I was at the mall, and, and…"

Jimmy looked like he was about to keel over. "Jimmy," I stood up and motioned toward my chair, "have a seat."

"Thanks coach." Jimmy took a deep breath. "So, like I was saying, I was at the mall and this old lady, she just starts yelling at me. I thought she was going to start whacking me with her purse."

"What'd you do to her?"

"Nothing coach."

I looked at Jimmy skeptically.

"I swear coach. She said I needed to be nicer to my elders. I tried to explain my shirt to her coach, but she wasn't having any of it."

A player jogged up next to Jimmy and patted him on the back. "'Seniors? We don't need no stinkin' Seniors.' Right Jimmy?"

I couldn't help but laugh. At least no one could say we didn't have an identity.

That season we met our goal. Not a single team blew us out on our way to a 3-6-1 record. It was the kind of year that you look back on as a stepping-stone along a path to greatness—a notion that was born out by their berth in the section title game the next year. The kids became "stinkin' seniors," and nearly won the whole thing. It was just without me.

The one thing that I can say about my one season at Golden Valley is that it was a success, with the only real hiccup coming against Merced. It wasn't that I expected us to beat them—they were a team stacked with seniors who knew how to win, or that I thought we could have played better that game. There isn't a coach alive that doesn't think that after *every* game. It was that everything seemed backwards. We were in the wrong locker room, we were on the wrong sidelines, and we were in the wrong colored uniforms. For that night, it even felt like I was coaching the wrong players. It was as close to an out-of-body experience as I have ever had. Having survived it, I am pretty sure that I don't ever want to have another one.

After the game, I found myself spending more time with my former players than with my current ones. The experience furthered my feeling that something was amiss—not necessarily with Merced or Golden Valley, but with me. Little things started to bother me more than they had before. I wasn't as excited as the other coaches to continue building the program through the off-season. I also didn't have my usual vigor in the classroom. It could have been that I had been scrambling to put together the 170 days worth of lessons that Sue and I had taught each year into a master's thesis. Subsequently, however, when the district denied the accreditation of the school through which I was working, Columbia Pacific University, I finally snapped.

I explained to the district that I had sought to get my master's degree at local universities three other times. Each time I had been told that I needed to take at least one semester off from teaching. I told them that not only was that financially impossible for me, but irresponsible as the head football coach and a teacher with a collection of students who relied on the stability provided by having the same two teachers being there every single day. Furthermore, I pointed out that I had selected Columbia Pacific University because it was accredited in the eyes of the state of California, as well as by 50 other associations nationally.

The district replied that all degrees had to be from colleges and universities accredited by the Western Association of Schools and Colleges (WASC), and they recommended that I try the program through Chapman University.

In the most candid moment that I have ever had with an authority figure, I told him that his recommendation was a scam. I knew that he taught in the Chapman University program and that I had attended one of his classes. It was boring and inapplicable, a ridiculous hoop on the obstacle course to a meaningless master's degree. What I had produced was valid documentation of a cutting-edge program that had actually worked to change students' lives. If that didn't represent the kind of growth and thought that the district wanted out of its "master teachers," then I didn't want to be considered one of them.

I was still steaming days later, when I got a phone call from Dan Hawkins that would change both my and my family's lives forever. I had gotten to know Dan through Phil Maas, the guy who had introduced me to the fly offense. Phil had become the head coach of College of the Siskiyous. On occasion, we'd gotten together to talk about the changes that I had made to the fly. For Phil, the fly was still just a component of his primarily veer offense, whereas for me, it was the exact opposite. As a result, we liked to periodically get together in hopes of diversifying both our own and each others' play calling.

Phil had hired Dan as an assistant, and from our first meeting, it was obvious why. The guy was on fire. He was a ball of energy and enthusiasm, dying for information and always ready with a question. He was the kind of coach that I would have loved to play for, as well as the kind of coach I would send my players to play for. In fact, he was the kind of coach I hoped I was. Frankly, I never thought we'd coach together. He had designs on coaching in a Super Bowl, while I had designs on getting my master's degree accepted by the school district. On the other hand, who was I to deny destiny? Besides, all I was doing was answering the phone.

When Dan called, I knew that he had moved on to a little school in the Pacific Northwest called Willamette because I had written a letter (upon his request) stating that I would recommend my players to any university at which he was the coach. Since I had met him, we talked pretty consistently about once a year. Sometimes, it was at a conference we were both attending. On occasion, it was at a clinic where we were both speaking. Sometimes, it was over the phone about a potential recruit. Accordingly, I was a bit surprised when he informed me about the topic of our conversation.

"What's up Dan?"

"You man. You're what's up."

"What do you mean?"

"Do you want to come be the offensive coordinator at Willamette?"

I had to fight off a coughing fit before I responded. "You're kidding."

"No, I'm not kidding."

He wasn't kidding.

He didn't talk salary, he didn't talk timeline, he just talked about how terrific it was, working with motivated kids in a place where he could look out his window and see 15 different species of trees and grass that stayed green all year long.

After our brief conversation, I walked down the hall and poked my head into Sue's office.

"Hey Sue, you want to go live in Oregon?"

"Really?" She turned in her chair and looked at me, knowing that over the last few days, I'd suggested moving to Honolulu, Boston, and Timbuktu—just so long as they would accept my degree.

I nodded. "Really."

"Okay."

❖ ❖ ❖

The next day, Dan called again, and he started to talk about the details of a potential move up to Oregon. Before we got too far into it, I told Dan that I knew universities wanted their coaches to all have master's degrees and that the local school district wouldn't even accept mine.

"You got a master's? Don't sweat it. We'll take it."

Our conversation ended with a tentative arrangement for Sue and I to fly up to Oregon and check out the school. When I hung up the phone, I wasn't thinking about what Salem might be like, or how the kids might take a move, I was thinking about what a bargaining chip Willamette's affirmation of my master's degree was. Rather than going home after work excited to talk to Sue about our upcoming trip, I drove down to the district office.

I strode into the HR director's office, and without any pleasantries, I explained my conversation with Dan and said, "So, you're telling me that one of the top small liberal arts universities in the country is going to accept my degree, and a school district where 20 percent of students qualify for the California state university system is not?" Frankly, my outpouring didn't go over very well.

After our trip up to Oregon, Sue and I spent a week going over the pros and cons of the move. We'd make less money, but our expenditures would be less. We'd uproot the kids, two of which were in high school (Lisa was a sophomore, Tim was a freshman), but they'd get to go to Willamette for free. We'd be leaving behind a population of students who needed our attention, but then, there might be more time for us as a family. We really were on the fence about the move. We needed something to tip the scale one way or another.

The next day, a story ran in the Merced newspaper about a 90-year-old man who had been fighting since the 1950s to get a golf course built in Merced. Finally, his wish was coming true. The photo on the front page showed the man in a hard hat with a shovel, as he was starting construction on the course. Only, it looked as if the shovel and dirt were too heavy for him to move. All he could do was stand, hunched over the ground that he had spent half his life trying to break. It brought to mind the stadium that I had tried to renovate, the funding that I had tried to receive, and the dishonored degree that I had worked hard to achieve. If we stayed in Merced, I was going to be that old man with that shovel, the school district's Sisyphus, pushing my rock up the hill. I had tried changing rocks, but the work was just as hard. I realized, sometimes you have to change hills.

We were moving to Oregon.

Chapter 20 The Grass Is Always Greener … or Is It?

I wouldn't say that Willamette University and Salem are in diametric opposition to Merced and the high school, but it's close. There aren't a lot of places in the world where a stream runs through the campus and baby ducklings can be seen racing in and among the sunbathing students every spring. There aren't a lot of places in the world where you can have a hawk looming over your agility drills, waiting for a squirrel to make a wrong move. Just as importantly, there aren't a lot of places where your administrators are your biggest fans.

To say that Willamette was a breath of fresh air for me was an understatement. The evening news didn't even bother to address the air quality during its weather report. Furthermore, nowhere was this situation more apparent than with the players.

It's not that I didn't love the kids that I had in Merced, because I did. To my utter surprise, the players at Willamette amazed me with their level of excitement—for their classes. They couldn't wait to talk about a lecture or a lab, and they were concerned about their grades. At Merced, it had been like pulling teeth to get them to admit they had homework. In Willamette, the players scheduled appointments with their professors, film sessions with coaches, and meeting times with tutors—or *as* them. When you greeted a player, he would offer a firm handshake. Furthermore, when you talked to him, every movement of your lips was tracked as if he was listening with his eyes. The players weren't just mature—they were regimented about being mature, an attribute that made practice as different from Merced as the guys practicing.

At Merced, warm-ups were done with militaristic precision. I led the stretching. Even though I would joke around throughout the routine, it was as if I was the happy drill sergeant—a joy to be around so long as everyone was in line and on task. My kids at Merced thrived in that sort of structure. Left to their own devices, the warm-ups would have been chaos.

At Willamette, the last thing the players needed was more structure. Instead, they needed to be able to cut themselves loose from chaos theory and create a bit of their own chaos. I, of course, didn't know this factor my first practice. As a result, I was more than a little shocked when coaches were playing catch through the stretch lines, laughing as they got intercepted by players, and making sure to razz every single player they could.

A younger version of me probably would have asked about the rationale behind distracting players as they prepared for practice. On the other hand, I had made a promise to myself when I arrived that I wasn't going to say anything unless I was asked. It was the best decision I made in those first three years. That didn't mean I wasn't a bit uncomfortable at first.

Shortly after I was hired, I discovered that not only was I going to have to coach a position that I'd never coached—offensive line—but I wasn't even Dan's top choice. In reality, I was somewhere around fourth, but being behind the likes of The University of Washington's current head coach, Chris Peterson, isn't so bad. Dan had also said that although he wanted to run the fly, he wanted to keep their current terminology. After speaking with another one of the people who had entertained taking the job before I'd accepted it, Chris Strausser (Boise State's running game coordinator at the time), I discovered that not only was the terminology I was inheriting foreign to me, but the techniques were as well. For example, the way they blocked sounded an awful lot like a zone scheme—nothing like the way my linemen at Merced had blocked. It didn't even seem like I was going to get to call the plays, the job for which an offensive coordinator lives. Still, I kept my mouth shut.

My first game during that 1995 season was against Central Washington, and I was up in the booth. In front of me, I had folders that I'd created about Central's tendencies, based on down-and-distance and the plays we liked, based on those tendencies. Before each down that first series, I relayed to Dan what I was seeing on the field. He would then ask what I thought we should call. He took every one of my suggestions. By the time the series was over, Dan asked if I wanted to call the game.

From that point on, the offense was mine. But, that was all that was mine.

Once the season got rolling, I was amazed at how much more energy I had than when I was at Merced. There were no classes to teach, there were no grades I had to check, there was no fundraising I had to do. All I had to do was worry about football. Furthermore, not just football—only the offense. Our defense was run by the immensely talented Bob Gregory, with assistance from his inimitable mentor Bob Foster. The last thing they needed was me to meddle in their affairs or even ask about what they were doing. I didn't even have to worry about program issues. For example, if a chinstrap got left on the field, either the player who lost it would be responsible enough to go find it or the equipment guy would put it away. I remember being asked on multiple occasions when the bus for Linfield was leaving and feeling perfectly comfortable with answering, "I don't know. Check with Coach Hawk."

It was terrific. Until I would get home.

One of the primary positive things about the move to Willamette was that Sue and I knew that it would be great for the kids. When it was time for them to go to college, they'd be able to go for free. On the other hand, none of them were in college yet. To be ripped away from their friends and their fledging social lives was difficult, especially on Lisa. She'd already established herself at school in Merced and to start over halfway through high school was hard for her, which, in turn, was hard for both Sue and me to see. The resulting circumstances created a troublesome situation. Sue was the only one available to talk to Lisa (or Tim or Julie), because I never knew when I'd be home.

During the season, this situation was especially difficult on Sundays through Wednesdays, because assistant coaches never knew when the meeting was going to end, and we never received permission to leave early. It seemed as if they would end on a whim—sometimes at 9:30 at night, sometimes at 12:30 in the morning. So, when Sue would call, anxious for help dealing with the hormone-filled house, I was unable to say when I would be home.

After the football season was over, the issue of when would I be home that night was no longer the question. The setting turned into when would I be home that *week*. Unlike high school, when the end of the football season meant the beginning of some breathing room, at Willamette, the end of football brought on the beginning of recruiting.

In high school, I'd done some recruiting of sorts. Frankly, it was a captive audience, and there weren't a lot of options—not a lot of big guys were itching to play the piccolo in the Merced marching band. So, when I got through that first season at Willamette and was given a region to recruit, I really had no idea what to do. My first instinct was pick up the community college course catalogue to see if they offered a class about it. I quickly dispelled that notion, however. Correspondence school was also out (I'd had enough of those). In reality, there were no classes to be taken anywhere on how to recruit.

As a result, I felt compelled to violate my personal pact, and I began to ask questions about what I should do. Everyone was more than willing to provide me with answers—if they were in town. Today, I might have just given them a call while they were on the road. Then, however, no one had cell phones. It was all landlines. In other words, you were either calling from home, from school, or from any phone you could find when you were out and about in your region.

I remember working on a visit to my dad during a California recruiting trip (it ended up being the last time I saw him), and having to cut it short, because I had a scheduled stop at a high school up Highway 17. It had been raining all day. By the time I figured out I was lost in Hecker Pass, it had turned into a deluge. I pulled onto the shoulder of an overpass and hunkered within the limited shelter of a half-covered payphone, as I tried to find the number for the high school before the ink of my notes washed away. When I finally managed to get the number dialed and someone answered, I had to scream over the downpour and the traffic, as well as dodge the occasional spray from passing semis.

I can't tell you if we got the player whom I called that day. I can tell you, however, that it was stops that like that that could shave time off a trip. This factor is critically important, because you never know when something else could slow you down—a delayed flight, a problem with the car rental, or a lost bag. The thing is, you want to do everything you can to avoid slowing yourself down. Such a goal, however, is not accomplished by speeding yourself up.

On one of my first out-of-town flights, I had scheduled it in the evening so that I could put in a full day of work at the school. I knew that I had a meeting early the next morning. Arriving in Seattle at 9:15, I knew that I had a 45-minute drive to the hotel. With an 8:00 appointment at a high school the next morning, I figured that if everything went smoothly, I could be in my room by 10:15, asleep by 11:00, and have the opportunity to get some decent rest. I hustled off the airplane, grabbed my bag, flew through the car rental line, and was at the front desk by 10:05 (I promise that it had nothing to do with my driving).

I usually insist that when I make reservations that I'm put in a regular room. I've figured out a lot in my life, but how to make the bars in the handicapped shower work for me is not one of them. Unfortunately, I hadn't made any request this trip, and they had me booked in handicapped accessible quarters. After inquiring about the availability of a regular room and discovering that the hotel was booked solid, I decided to make the best of my situation. I was still going to be able to get to sleep early, and on trips like these, that was all you could ask for.

When I walked into my room, I tossed my bag on the bed. I had the urge to just flop on top of the comforter and fall asleep, but I fought it off. Instead, I figured I could get shaving out of the way that night and buy a couple more minutes of shut-eye in the morning. I set about rifling through the bag in search of my razor. Between the aroma of lilacs and the feel of silk, however, I was pretty sure I wasn't going to be finding my Barbasol® in that bag. I'd grabbed the wrong suitcase.

I made the drive back to the airport, and after finding a spot in short-term parking, speaking with a baggage attendant, making the exchange, winding my way out of the lot, navigating Seattle traffic, and getting back to my room, I discovered the entire trip had taken just shy of two and a half hours—twice the time as my flight from Oregon. It was close to one in the morning. It dawned on me that not only was I going to have to explain to a bunch of high school players about where Willamette University was located and how a guy with no hands came to be a coach there, I was also going to have to do it with bags under my eyes and razor burn on my neck.

It was just a fact of life for the itinerant college football coach. As a college coach, however, you understood that you never knew where your job would take you. What I didn't realize was that extended beyond recruiting. Even when I was in the office, it seemed that every other conversation was about where people were going to find their next job. From the moment I'd known Dan, I'd known he was ambitious. Subsequently, I discovered that the third full-time coach, Bob Gregory, was also ambitious.

Every week seemed to bring a new machination, whereby one of our staff would get a job and move on to bigger and better things. This situation struck me as odd, because though while I knew it could get bigger than Willamette, it didn't seem like it could get much better. I began to get more comfortable with the situation in my second year at Willamette, because our offense had really started to hum. In reality, it seemed like an unspoken truth that if Dan got picked up by somebody, he'd take Bob, me, and the entire staff with him.

After my third season, Dan and Bob did leave Willamette … just not together. And I stuck around.

During my third year, 1997, we set school records on both sides of the ball, with several players receiving All-American recognition. It was also notable that Willamette memorabilia was being sent to the College Football Hall of Fame in honor of the first woman—Liz Heaston—to play in a college football game (she was one of our kickers). We made a run to the national title game, losing 14-7, without our All-American quarterback Chuck Pinkerton. Because Dan had narrowly missed on getting a head job at a Division 1-AA school the year before, when we'd only made it to the second round of the playoffs, it wasn't much of a stretch to think that he might get another opportunity after that season. That season, however, we'd been so focused on trying to win each week that it seemed as if all of the typical "who's going where" chatter had died down.

On the plane ride back from Tennessee, the venue for the title game, everyone was exhausted and in their own world. Coaches were getting sleep for the first time in weeks, and players were taking the finals that they'd missed while they were away. There wasn't a word of football spoken by anyone. The next day, the players turned their gear in to the coaches, who stuck around for a short meeting afterwards to discuss everyone's recruiting regions. Then, Dan told us all to take a week off. The date was December 18.

On December 19, I snuck into work, knowing that the only way to start recruiting is to simply start recruiting. No one else was around, which shouldn't have been a surprise, except for the absence of Dan, who always worked even when he gave us time off. I shrugged it off, figuring that he'd decided to sleep in and would just be in later that day.

About an hour later I heard a knock on my door. It was Bill Trenbeath, our athletic director.

Dan wasn't going to be coming into the office today. Or ever again. He'd taken a job at Boise State as an assistant head coach, effective immediately.

"Mark, we want to move fast to hire a new head coach."

"Oh." Visions of what that search might look like began to take murky form in my brain.

"We want you to be our head coach."

I coughed. "What about Bob?"

"Bob doesn't want it. Besides, you've got head coaching experience."

"I see."

"Talk it over with Sue. And, say hi to her for me."

I began to picture that conversation in my head. It wasn't pretty. We'd already had a number of discussions about what I could do to be home more and to help with the kids more. I couldn't imagine having more time at home as the head coach. On the other hand, Lisa had managed to graduate from high school and had decided to attend Willamette. Tim would be graduating soon too. He might even be able to play at Willamette. I would be giving up a job I loved, a job where I didn't have to worry about the logistical nightmare of running a football program, only the offense I had designed. What would we do, however, if I didn't take the position? If the new coach came in with his own staff and cleaned house, I'd be out of a job, Lisa's tuition-free education would be gone, Tim's opportunity to play for his dad would be gone, and we'd be looking to move wherever the fickle coaching wind happened to blow that year.

We discussed the options as a family and decision came back unanimous. I was going to be a head coach again.

Chapter 21 Still Figuring It Out

It's hard to believe that I'd been the head coach of Willamette for 10 years. Furthermore, I hadn't even managed to wear out my welcome. It feels as if it's been the fastest decade in history. The thing is, although I'm sure that I'm out on the recruiting trail this very minute searching for the next great fly guy, if it were to all end today, I could look back on my life and appreciate its symmetry.

In some ways, I can see my life as having perfect bookends:

- The first coaching job I ever had, I was surprised in my third week when I was asked to become the head coach. In my last coaching job, I was surprised in my third year when I was asked to become the head coach.

In other ways, I can see my life as a mirror, a reflection of my parent's lives:

- My father raised a son to love football by immersing him within the sport and surrounding him with people who played with a passion. I too raised my son to love football, but where my dad only got to watch me as a fan, I got to see Tim play as his coach, and coach as his colleague.
- My mother had her kids with one man and found a life partner with another, yet somehow managed to make sure her kids always knew she'd do anything she could to keep their dreams alive. Sue and I have not only managed to see Tim become a coach, but we have seen Julie and Lisa move to New York in eager pursuit of their own futures.

But mostly, however, I see my life as a circle. I say that because, in some ways, I feel like the dog an owner has tied to a post in the front yard. No matter where he goes, how fast he runs, or what direction he heads, he'll never get further from that post than he's supposed to. My post was put in the ground a long time ago. The factor around which my life would revolve was my family. No matter the age, the stage, or the place, I was always firmly grounded, thanks to that deep-seeded value.

Now one should conclude that I didn't try to run. It seems as if I was always running, running in pursuit of the same thing: a desire to be the best at whatever I did. This situation didn't mean as a person with no hands; it meant as a person *period*. Early on in my life, that meant I was going to have to show the world that I could do everything that they could, only better. That's what led me to sports and kept me in music. That's why I needed to get rid of the hooks. They weren't a tool. They were a crutch, and they slowed me down.

The one time that my hooks would have ever been of assistance to me was before one of the rare fights in my life—in fourth grade. Even then, I got rid of them. I didn't want to be seen as having an advantage. Mike had stepped between the bully and me, and as I struggled to get out of my brother's grasp, I heard the kid taunt, "besides, it wouldn't be fair fighting 'Captain Hook.'" For a moment, Mike relaxed his grip, and I raised a hook to the top of my flannel shirt. With one swipe, I ran it down the front, popping off every button. I took a step back from Mike, and, with a couple of violent shakes from my shoulders, I was free from both the shirt and the prostheses. At that point, Mike saw what was about to happen, and he moved out of the way. Three steps and one swing later, the bully had been decked. Captain Hook my ass.

My drive to be the best, with or without hands, drove me all the way through college. By the time I graduated, however, there was nothing about my lack of hands that could potentially hold me back. Instead, I had to figure out how to be the best husband, the best father, the best teacher, the best coach, and the best fundraiser I could be. Furthermore, I was going to have to figure it out the same way everyone else did. I was also going to have to determine new ways forward. In turn, when I reached the end of my leash, I realized that I had two choices—keep pulling the same way I'd been pulling, go nowhere, and have the exact same view, or change direction and see something different.

Every time I've reached the end of that leash, I've changed directions—eventually. But if you keep turning and keep adjusting, eventually you're going to end up back where you started. That's what happened to me when I came to Willamette. I am back to being a head coach, I am back to living in an empty nest, and strangely enough, I am back to fighting the same battle I did when I was a kid—fighting against my lack of hands.

In some ways, it's the same as it was then. I play racquetball with fellow coaches, players, even the co-author of this book. All factors considered, I expect to beat them every time. In other ways, however, it's different. I never expected to have a profession where I would be recruiting confident young men, who wouldn't know what to say when their potential head coach entered a handshake without a hand. In many ways, I've tried to embrace my particular set of unique circumstances. For example, I love to drive recruits around in a manual transmission. On the other hand, sometimes, it seems the situation is winning (I'm still trying to figure out how I'm supposed to electronically check-in at airports using my credit card).

This point is where the dog-run analogy breaks down. As such, the dog is usually going so fast that the view never really changes when he gets back around to where he started. You might say that, in that way, the earth's orbit around the sun is more appropriate. In other words, it takes a year for a cycle to become complete, and the bounds of gravity are invisible (plus, I'm sure that Sue, the kids, my mom, and my siblings would prefer to being thought of as a gravitational pull on a leash). It also seems a bit pompous to compare myself to a celestial body. Besides, it too doesn't quite fit. If there's anything I've learned in this life, it's that while people don't change, their perspectives do. Frankly, the earth's view of the sun doesn't seem to have changed much in my time on the planet.

In that way, I would say that my life most closely matches the "hero circle" that Lisa, Julie, and Tim told me about from their English classes at South Salem High School. Like those heroes, I had guides to help me on my way. Like those heroes, I have had to overcome obstacles. Furthermore, like those heroes, I have married the girl and returned to where I've begun.

In reality, if you think about it, that's probably your story too. It is also the story of millions of other people. I suppose that means that it is up to you to decide if you're a hero or what it would take for you or anybody else to be considered one.

As for me, I don't think I'm a hero. I'm just a guy trying to make his way in the world—in shoes that somebody else tied.

Epilogue

Many changes have occurred in my life since the first edition of this book was published in 2010. The biggest change has been in my football life. Before the 2012 season, I left Willamette University to become the head coach at Menlo College, one of my alma maters. A phone call out of the blue from Keith Spataro, the athletic director at Menlo, started the whole ball rolling. Suddenly, we were leaving the familiar confines of Salem Oregon for the San Francisco Bay Area, a place in which I hadn't lived for almost 40 years. Surely, someone somewhere remarked that I left the Willamette program in better hands than mine.

This was a big change for Sue and me. I was excited to help rebuild a struggling Menlo football program. Working for Keith, getting reacquainted with old friends, and changing the culture of the team was a great opportunity, and I loved it. Sue enjoyed exploring a new area, and we both loved the sunny days in the winter, especially when we knew it was raining in Salem. Then, another phone call out of the blue changed our trajectory.

Dan Hawkins, who had hired me way back at Willamette, was on the phone. "Hey Speck, if Marc Trestman gets the head coaching job with the Chicago Bears, I have a chance to replace him as the head coach at Montreal! You interested?" I had a hard time following him. "Did you say Montreal?" I asked. I wasn't sure that they even had a football team. "Yes," he replied, "the Montreal Alouettes. They are a pro team in the Canadian Football league." He went on to extoll the virtues of coaching pro football, living in French-speaking Montreal for six months, and running the fly offense with Canadian rules. "Mark, in Canada, everyone can be in motion, not just one player, like in American football. Imagine all of the creative ways we could use that to make the fly offense go!"

I had to admit, it was an intriguing idea. "If you get the job, I'd be interested" was my reply. When we hung up the phone, I dismissed the idea for two reasons. One, it was crazy. I'd just been at Menlo for one season, and was looking forward to seeing how much improvement we could make in the coming season. And two, there was no way Dan, with no professional experience, would get the job.

A few weeks later, I had to make a decision. Go to Montreal. Or stay at Menlo. Dan called. He got the job and wanted me to coach the running backs. It was an agonizing decision. I hated the idea of leaving Menlo. On the other hand, the prospect of coaching professional football and living in Montreal was an opportunity that doesn't come your way very often. Sue and I agonized over the decision. After much thought and prayer, we decided to take the Montreal job. How could we pass up this adventure?

In the last two years, I discovered that pro football players were just like the high school and college players with whom I'd worked. At first, they were surprised to see a coach with no hands on the staff. With very little fanfare, I started coaching them up. They asked about my hands, I told them I was born without them, and we moved on. After a few days of throwing passes to them, catching their throws, working the computer in meetings, and writing on the white board, my circumstance was a non-issue. As I proved my competency as a coach on the field and in meetings, only the occasional joke at my expense reminded anyone of my situation.

While my professional life has changed a lot, some things remain very constant for me. I am still different looking than most people. I am still the coach/speaker/guy without hands. I still need to constantly *figure out* daily situations in my life. Frankly, I have practiced this skill for so long, I am confident I will be able to handle any situation that comes along.

I have *figured out* that there are some great benefits to my life in front of the public. I have witnessed firsthand, (no pun intended), how people representing all races, creeds, and colors universally have the instinct to offer help and kindness to me. Time after time, I have witnessed the good in people.

I have also had the opportunity to provide hope or comfort to people facing their own loss of a limb, or to parents of children who have some type of handicap. I have come to understand that my *figuring* things *out* is important for me, but ultimately, also is a way for me to pay it forward. I have come to learn that I must constantly strive to reach my potential, and by doing so, pass the lessons on to others. In that regard, I have encountered a number of examples.

In Montreal, for example, Sue and I met a vibrant, elderly couple through some mutual friends. We had several social occasions with Barbara and Murray, and each time, I remarked what a great zest for life they possessed. Murray was battling cancer, and had seemed to have beaten it. The week before we were to leave Montreal, however, word got to us that Murray's cancer had returned and that the doctors felt his only chance was the amputation of his left arm just above the elbow.

The night before the surgery, we talked on the phone. What can you say at a time like this? I tried humor first, "Murray, you know, this is a really effective weight loss technique!" We laughed a bit, and then it became serious. I reassured him he had the ability to *figure it out*, and he'd quickly learn to adapt.

Like my mom did for me, I listed all that he still had going for him. The arm being amputated was his non-dominant hand. The doctors felt certain that the cancer was confined to his arm being amputated. He had an outstanding team of therapists ready to help him adjust. Murray remarked that "the therapist said you can drive with one hand, that there is a device you can use, do you think that's true?" I laughed and said, "I've been driving with no hands for 41 years, so it'll be a breeze for you with one! There is a device you can put on the steering wheel that allows people to drive one-handed." Murray responded, "That's good to know." Just before we hung up, Murray said, "Mark, you have really had a blessed life. It is remarkable. I know I can do this."

Now, Murray, even at 84, has to continue to reach his potential and *figure out* his next life challenge. I am struck that we never totally reach our potential. We never stop *figuring it out*. There is always more we can accomplish. It is what life is about.

I received an email from a colleague at work, whose nephew had had his feet and hands amputated in a lifesaving operation right after birth. My colleague asked what advice I would give the parents. I did not respond right away, as I was trying to *figure out* what I could possibly tell these parents. As I thought about this situation, it struck me that all my life experiences had prepared me to give my unique perspective to this family. I needed to encapsulate the important lessons learned, while being hopeful, yet truthful. I needed to *figure out* how to give some light in a dark situation. I hope this note gave them some comfort. I hope my experiences help him on his journey. I hope they understand we all have unlimited potential and the ability to *figure it out*. The following is what I wrote…:

Dear Janet,

I am very sorry to hear about the situation your nephew is in, and my heart goes out to the parents. I also apologize for the tardiness in responding. I have given this situation a lot of thought, and wanted my answer to convey the right tone and message.

What advice would I have for the family?

I would tell them to not lose faith. God has a plan, and it is going to work out.

I would tell them to be thankful he is an infant, as he will use his innate ability to *figure it out* and adapt to his situation. I have a friend who lost his feet and hands to frostbite. It is much tougher to *figure it out* as an adult, than as an infant. While my friend did *figure it out* and adapted, it was more difficult for him.

I would tell them that there is no room for self-pity. I would tell them don't baby him or allow him to use his situation as an excuse. He will need to be tough. The parents need to teach him. Make him do chores. Make him write. Make him play. If he has siblings, hold them all to the same standards.

Don't fear failure. He will learn to do things in ways that will amaze. But there will be some breathtaking, scary, and sad failures along the way. They will teach him and pave the way for success.

I would tell them that he will want to be normal and do normal things. He will have a drive that will help him survive. He will not want to be singled out or given any special treatment. Yet, the ironic truth is that as he adapts, he will bring more attention to himself. Because to the average person, anything he accomplishes will be amazing. The sooner he learns that he has a unique purpose and has been called to a unique life, the sooner he will feel comfortable sharing his story. For me, that didn't happen until after college.

I would tell them that doctors will have a lot of good information and ideas, but to let the child intuitively *figure out* his situation. The advances in prosthetic feet and legs are remarkable. The advances are not as good with hands and arms. Get him upright and walking as soon as possible, but closely watch how quickly and adeptly he uses his arms. He may not need anything to replace his hands. Utilize the best science can offer, but let him lead the way. He will know what feels right or wrong.

Teach him that there are no limits. Find his passion, and get out of his way. He can flourish. He will have a full and rich life. It will be different, and at times heartbreaking, but isn't that true with all kids?

I would tell them God has a plan, and from the worst tragedies, come God's best work. It is going to be a great adventure.

Appendix Photos Through the Years

As a player at Menlo junior college

As a player at Azusa Pacific University

Making a tackle at Azusa Pacific (#10)

Merced High School 1989 section championship team

Coaching at Merced High School

On the field with Merced players

Giving last-minute instructions to players before a game at Willamette University

Celebrating a Willamette victory

Receiving a victory shower from Willamette players

Giving a congratulatory fist bump to a Willamette player

Drawing up a play on the sidelines during a game

Making sideline adjustments during a game at Willamette

Talking to a Willamette player

As the new Menlo College head football coach

At a press conference, being introduced as the new Menlo College head football coach

Coaching for the Montreal Alouettes

At the Alouettes spring camp

Conducting running back drills with the Alouettes

Practicing with the Alouettes

Celebrating Mother's Day with mom and brother Matt

Enjoying free time with wife Sue

About the Authors

Before becoming a professional football coach, Mark Speckman was the head football coach at the collegiate level for 15 years. At NCAA Division III Willamette University in Salem, Oregon, Mark lead the Bearcats to an impressive 82-59 (.582) record, including an outstanding 47-28 (.627) record in Northwest Conference play. Additionally, Willamette enjoyed five conference championships, five national playoff berths, and a 1997 national championship game appearance.

In 2008, Speckman was a Liberty Mutual National Coach of the Year finalist, where he was featured on ABC and ESPN. He is also regarded as an authority on the fly offense. Speckman spent two seasons suiting up as linebacker for Menlo from 1973–74, and was inducted into the Menlo College Athletic Hall of Fame in 2009. After the '74 season, Speckman transferred to Azusa Pacific University in Azusa, California to complete his degree. In the process, he earned NAIA All-American Honorable Mention honors as a player. In 2004, the Oregonian newspaper named Speckman on their list of the 25 most influential sports figures in the state of Oregon. In 2007, Mark was inducted into the Peninsula Sports Hall of Fame as a coach and an athlete.

What's most impressive, however, is that Mark accomplished all of this despite being born without hands. Mark learned early on that he couldn't escape his disability. He had to face his challenges and *figure* life *out* without hands. In his mid-20s, Mark made a pact with God to use his disability to create a positive impact on the lives of others. He made a promise to share his life story with anyone who inquired. Since then, Mark has been featured by numerous national media outlets (including ESPN and *USA Today*) and has established himself as one of the most in-demand motivational speakers in the country.

While Mark's physical disability is evident, his message is about helping people recognize and overcome the "disabilities" in their own life. At the end of the day, all of us are limited by disabilities that keep us from realizing our potential. Whether it is poor communication skills, a fear of failure, or a lack of organization, we all have weaknesses in our lives that require extra effort or creativity on our part to achieve success. Mark's story is not about avoiding life's twists and turns or hiding from our weaknesses. Rather, it is about conditioning one's self to believe in the power of the human spirit and achieve our highest goals.

Mark is a professional motivational speaker. He can be reached at speckmanspeaks.com

W. Jason Niedermeyer is a high school teacher, a husband, and a father of two boys. He is the author of several short stories and recently earned his doctorate in education from George Fox University. He intends to someday teach pre-service teachers at a college in the Pacific Northwest.